Socio-Economic Base-Line Survey of Rural and Urban Households in Tana Sub-Basin, Amhara National Regional State

Kassahun Berhanu & Tegegne Gebre-Egziabher

FSS Monograph No. 10

Forum for Social Studies (FSS)
Addis Ababa

Printed in Addis Ababa

Typesetting & Layouts: Konjit Belete

ISBN: 13: 978-99944-50-49-7

Forum for Social Studies (FSS)
P.O. Box 25864 code 1000
Addis Ababa, Ethiopia
Email: fss@ethionet.et
Web: www.fssethiopia.org.et

This monograph has been published with the financial support of the Civil Societies Support Program (CSSP). The contents of the monograph are the sole responsibilities of the authors and can under no circumstances be regarded as reflecting the position of the CSSP or the FSS.

Table of Contents

List of Tables

Acronyms

BOFED	Bureau of Finance and Economic Development
FHHs	Female-headed household/s
FTC	Farmers' Training Center
FSS	Forum for Social Studies
HCs	Health clinic/s
HHs	Household/s
HPs	Health post/s
MoFED	Ministry of Finance and Economic Development
PASDEP	Plan for Accelerated and Sustained Development to End Poverty

I. INTRODUCTION

1.1 Background and Statement of the Problem.

The Tana watershed located in the Amhara National Regional State constitutes one of the sub-basins of the Blue Nile along with the Beles sub-basin located in the Benishangul-Gumuz Region. It is estimated that a total population of over 3 million people inhabit the Tana and Beles sub-basins that vary in terms of population density, ethnic composition, livelihood systems, and socio-cultural norms.

The Tana sub-basin, which is the object of this baseline survey, is largely inhabited by members of the Amhara ethnic group. In terms of livelihood system, the Amharas inhabiting the Tana sub-basin conduct sedentary farming that is complemented with limited livestock production. In terms of resources, the Tana-sub basin alone commands significant agricultural potential that could boost efforts aimed at augmenting commercial and smallholder agricultural production.

According to MoFED (2006), the two sub-basins together form one of the five 'growth corridors' in the country due to their endowment in water resources that can be used for engaging in rain-fed and irrigated farming by taking advantage of the existing productive land and a relatively developed infrastructure that has a potential for accessing market outlets. The Tana-Beles Growth Corridor is the first of its kind in Ethiopia that became the focus of government policy as outlined by MoFED (2006). The corridor is envisaged to:

- accelerate rates of growth and economic development;
- form part of a geographically differentiated growth strategy for exploiting existing endowments characterized by distinct agro-ecological characteristics and natural resources;
- effect linkages between agriculture and industry; and
- attract the private sector as the driver of growth supported by a conducive policy and institutional environment and improved infrastructure.

The core driver of initiating the growth corridor is associated with the urge for developing land and water resources with emphasis on transforming and expanding the present land and water -based economic sectors (Ministry of water resources, 2008). The existing resource endowment of the Sub-Basin is the main driver of the growth corridor leading to the identification of resource-based sectors or economic catalysts. These resource-based economic catalysts in the sub-basin under study include agriculture, agro-processing, fishery and tourism. On the basis of their availability, five growth zones are identified within the growth corridor as indicated below:

Table 1.1: Growth Zones in the Tana-Beles Growth Corridor

Growth zones	Location
Bahirdar and hinterland	Bahirdar
Megech	Gorgora-Gondar
Upper Beles	Pawe-Fendika-Gilgel Beles
Fogera	Woreta-DebreTabor
Lower Beles	Mankush

Numerous development interventions are underway in the Tana-Beles sub-basin in general and in the Tana sub-basin in particular. These include various irrigation schemes, hydropower production[1], watershed management, and prudent development and utilization of natural resources. The followings sections describe development interventions and their status at the time of writing this base line study specific to the Tana sub-basin

The Tana-Beles Integrated Water Resource Development Project

This is essentially a land and water resource development project that has three main components, which are provided hereunder along with the associated costs (Ministry of water resources, 2008):

A. Sub-Basin Resources Planning and Management ($17.61 million)

1. Water resource information systems development ($11.66 million)
2. Resource planning and management capacity building ($5.95million)

B. Natural Resource Management Investment ($40.83million)

[1] With regard to hydro power, the inter-basin transfer scheme connecting Lake Tana with the Beles Sub-Basin supplies water for hydropower in Upper-Beles where 460 MW of electricity is produced. It is envisaged that the inter-basin transfer based on the huge volume of water available in the Beles Sub-Basin will pave the way for further development of the area leading to growing interest for undertaking irrigated farming. A sugar factory has already started operations by planting sugarcane on a trial basis and investors have already embarked on exploring possibilities for developing aquaculture by taking note of the favorable conditions like high temperature and reliable flow from the hydropower plant. Expansion of other sugar estates on 18,000 ha in the area between Pawe and Fendika is also already underway.

1. Watershed management ($35.08 million)
2. Flood Management ($5.75 million)

C. Growth Oriented Investment Facilitation ($9.17 million)

1. Development Agency Support ($1.43million)
2. Growth-Oriented Investment Preparation ($7.74million)

While the Amhara Regional Bureau of Water Resources coordinates the overall project and is responsible for undertaking Component A of the project, different institutions are responsible regarding the implementation of the other components. For example, the watershed management component is undertaken by the Regional Bureau of Agriculture while the Flood management program is undertaken by the Regional Office of Food Security. Component C is implemented by the Regional Bureau of Finance and Economic Development (BOFED). It should also be noted that the total cost of the project is US $70 million, of which the World Bank is committed to provide US$ 45 million (Ministry of water resource, 2008).

The water resource project includes the development of water information system, building the capacity of stakeholders, and establishing the Abay River Authority. This project is implemented by the water resource authority. The watershed management component covers three areas, namely i) natural resource management, ii) livelihood intervention, and iii) project management (Ministry of water resources, 2008). The natural resource element has certain entry points, which include addressing the common problems that beneficiary communities encounter in the course of carrying out activities by encouraging them to actively involve in the bid for addressing their needs related to health, school, water and infrastructure. The project attempts to provide for community needs in these areas while at the same time encouraging beneficiaries to voluntarily participate in natural resource management and conservation without expecting any compensation for the contributions that they are expected to make. This approach avoids the previous mode of participating in natural resource management through Food for Work or Cash for Work. The livelihood intervention element includes using Farmer Training Centers (FTCs) that train farmers for a given period of time in familiarizing them with different technologies. Most FTCs are not currently functional in terms of providing training to farmers. The livelihood component also involves crop and livestock improvement. In the latter case, the focus would be on animal feed and animal health.

The watershed management component is undertaken in the localities along the Rib, Gumaro and Jema Rivers embracing a total of 82 micro-watersheds. Some of the activities that have been undertaken since the inception of the project in a time span of two years include activities associated with water conservation and forestry and agro-forestry including seedling stations. Community watershed plans are also developed in addition to designing watershed monitoring and evaluation system, which is undertaken by Finish bilateral aid that also deals with sediment concentration, sediment yield, water discharge, and socio-economic monitoring, among others.

Irrigation Schemes

Poor utilization and non-availability of water is the main constraint that entails food insecurity adversely affecting many farmers in Ethiopia. Dependence on rain-fed agricultural practices has limited farmers to producing only once a year. The poor state of reliability and variability of rainfall also constrain the production capacity of farmers. In this connection, it is to be noted that undertaking commercial agriculture in the area under study is also dependent on its availability during the dry seasons thereby necessitating the launching of irrigation schemes. At present, irrigation in the Tana sub-basin like in the localities in and around Beles is limited to recession irrigation mainly around Lake Tana where small-scale irrigation is commonly practiced. The small-scale irrigation schemes in the two sub-basins are estimated to cover only 1300 hectares at present. It is in view of this that the irrigation projects are mainly aimed at alleviating water shortages affecting smallholder farmers and possibly large-scale agricultural schemes are also affected in likewise manner. Different irrigation schemes are envisaged to be realized in the Tana-Beles sub-basins some of which are in the process of being implemented by the government while others are supported by multilateral donors, such as the World Bank.

Rib and Megech-Seraba Irrigation Projects

These irrigation schemes are found in the Tana sub-basin and are supported by the Ethio-Nile Irrigation and Drainage Project funded by the World Bank that allocated US $100 million for the period between 2008 and 2015.

Rib Irrigation Scheme

In the Rib Project Area, the arrangement is that the government constructs the dam while the World Bank-funded Ethio-Nile Irrigation and Drainage Scheme covers costs associated with putting in place the necessary infrastructure in the form of primary, secondary and tertiary canals. It is envisaged that the Rib irrigation scheme will develop 14,460 hectares of land through surface irrigation (Ministry of water resource, 2010 b). According to the interview held with the Director of the Ethio-Nile Project at Bahirdar, about 40% of the construction was completed in 2012. At the time of writing the report, the World Bank was running a bidding process for the construction of the irrigation canals that will take place following the completion of the dam construction phase.

The Megech-Seraba Project

The Project is a pumping scheme aimed at drawing water from Lake Tana and transported through pipe to a reservoir located 20 kms. away. This scheme is planned to develop 5,224 hectares of land for which the Ethio-Nile Project will cover costs for all the civil work including the building of reservoirs and different canals. The civil work for Megech irrigation project started in October 2012. The Project is envisaged to be completed in three years time. At the time of collecting the data for this study, it was reported that the first phase of the Project that is expected to irrigate 1000 hectares of land will be completed in one and half years' time. Construction is underway by a Chinese company while the supervision is undertaken by a French company, which will run the operation and maintenance of the irrigation scheme upon its completion for the subsequent five years.

The total irrigable land through pumping and surface water flow in the Tana basin is 20,000 hectares (World Bank, 2010). Three *woredas* namely Libo-kemekem, Fogera and Dembia in North and South Gondar Zones of the Amhara Region are included in these irrigation schemes of the northern Tana Basin. Currently, three years of the project lifecycle has already elapsed and most of the allocated funds for this will continue to be used for covering costs related to civil works.

Following their completion, the schemes are envisaged to make water available for smallholder farmers who are expected to pay fees for the water that they use. It is envisaged the each farmer will be given irrigable land of between 0.5 and 1 hectare in size after measures for consolidating and redistributing land are finalized. It was learnt that the schemes will entail displacing and resettling farmers who are required to leave their holdings in order to make way for the construction of the necessary irrigation infrastructures. As a result, about 2041 people will be affected or displaced and be included to those who will make use of the irrigated land. Land for accommodating those affected will be made available by reducing 20% of the previous holdings of the unaffected farmers in the Project area. In addition, arrangements are made for compensating the affected farmers who lost their houses and other property due to the implementation of the projects. To this end, there is a resettlement action plan which is already prepared. The action plan identifies farmers to be displaced and the amount of compensation needed. Accordingly, the government has earmarked a total amount of 30,000,000 birr for compensating affected farmers.

In general, it is expected that 12600 farmers will be beneficiaries from the schemes in question.

After the completion of activities associated with infrastructure development, the operation and management of the irrigation will be handled over to a private company that will be charged with the task of collecting water fee from farmers and run the overall operational management of the schemes. Once the cost for putting in place the irrigation projects is recovered in this manner, the responsibility for running the schemes will be transferred to the beneficiary communities through water users' associations that are to be established.

- **Upper and Lower Beles Irrigation Schemes**

The irrigation schemes located in Upper and Lower Beles are designed in such a way as to enable making use of the water that flows from the Tana-Beles Hydropower Project, which is discharged after generating hydropower. The water discharged in this manner enters the Beles River to be used for irrigating about 80,000 hectares of land in Upper and Lower Beles. The irrigable land covered in this scheme will be used both by smallholders and large-scale commercial farmers. There are five *woredas* in the upper Beles scheme of which four are in the Amhara region and one is in Metekel Zone of the Benishangul-Gumuz Region. The *woredas* are North Achefer, South Achefer, Dangila and Jawi, Alefa and Taqusa in Amhara, and Dangur in Metekel Zone of Benishangul-Gumuz Region. This project is supported by the Ethio-Nile Project, which is currently in the process of preparing a feasibility study. At present, there is no concrete information regarding the possible size and location of commercial and smallholder agricultural schemes. However, it is envisaged that the commercial farms may be required to cover part of the costs for the laying of infrastructure and pay water fees when they become operational.

- **The Koga Irrigation Scheme**

This scheme is designed to irrigate a total land area of 6,000 hectares and involves the construction of a dam and the associated canals (AFDB, 2001). Nearly 76% of the civil work is completed and the scheme is designed to make water available for smallholder farmers of the area (personal communication). Land consolidation and redistribution will be part of the irrigation scheme in order to make irrigable areas accessible to all farmers.

Koga irrigation Project is located in Mecha *woreda* of Amhara and is administered by the Abay River Basin Authority. Farmers in nine *kebeles* are targeted to benefit from the scheme, which covers 12 blocks and 11 night reservoirs. The irrigated land under each block ranges from 864 hectares to 290 hectares and in total the irrigation scheme can irrigate 7,004 hectares of land with additional extension of 200 hectares. About 10,000 household heads are to benefit from this project. The current land holding of each household in the project area varies between 0.5 to 3 hectares. This refers to holdings after 20% reduction for adjustment made to compensate land used for developing the irrigation infrastructure.

The irrigation scheme has four canals: primary, secondary, tertiary and quaternary. Each secondary canal serves one block where one association of irrigation users is to be formed by farmers themselves bringing the total to 12. In each tertiary canal a zone will be formed where there would be a total of 93 irrigation zones for the 93 tertiary irrigation canals. One water user's team is organized under each quaternary canal covering 16 hectares of irrigable land, which means that a total of 169 water teams will be formed in the Koga project. The water teams are responsible for observing schedules for making use of the water by members. For instance, every hectare of land receives water for 12 hours once every eight days. The water teams ensure that such schedules are strictly observed. In addition, the water teams distribute agricultural inputs to members and communicate with the extension workers. The major crops grown in the area include potato, wheat, maize, barley, vegetables (carrot, cabbage, tomato, onions), and pulses such as beans and peas.

Though the Project started operation three years ago, the irrigation scheme became fully functional about a year ago. According to the head of Mecha *woreda* agriculture office where the Project is located, farmers who embarked on irrigated agricultural production earlier are better in their water use, land preparation, use of improved seeds, and construction of furrows. The *woreda* agricultural officer believes that there has been increase in income of agricultural producers as a result of which they have started to own assets in the form urban houses, improved breeds of livestock, cycles, and horse-drawn carts.

- **Other Irrigation Schemes**

In addition to the aforementioned, other irrigation schemes supported by the government include Gumera, Jema, and Gilgel-Abay, whose purposes along with the previous schemes are shown below (Table 1.2):

Table 1.2: Dams in the Tana-Beles Growth Corridor and their various purposes

Dam	Irrigation	Flood mitigation	Water supply	Hydropower
Koga	X			
Gilgel-Abbay	X			X
Gumera	X	X		X
Jema	X	X		X
Megech	X	X	X	X
Rib	X	X		
Lower-Beles (Dangur)	X			X

SOURCE: Ministry of Water Resources (2010a)

Expected Changes in the Tana Beles Sub-Basins

The complex development intervention underway in the Tana-Beles sub-basins is expected to result in significant socio-economic changes, which could be multidimensional in nature as indicated below:

1. The irrigation projects are hoped to make water available to farmers and result in increased production and productivity thereby improving the livelihood of the people due to augmented income of beneficiary communities;
2. Social development in the form of better health and education services, and access to water for various uses resulting in livelihood improvement particularly for households in the project areas;
3. The way the irrigation projects are to be managed entail land consolidation and redistribution, which in turn implies resettlement measures in order to accommodate farmers that would be displaced by the project. It also implies a change in land ownership and land use/tenure system in the area. Concomitant to the resettlement, the issue of compensation that has to be commensurate with the loss of farmers is likely to be incurred as a result of expediting the irrigation schemes;
4. Large-scale farming taking place in the project areas imply agricultural production for export necessitating the formation of market outlets and the putting in place of physical infrastructure. It goes without saying that physical infrastructure will increase accessibility of the area while market outlets enable farmers to easily connect with regional, national and international commercial centers;

5. Land and utilization of water resources in the region requires the protection of the environment in order to help realize utilization of the full potential of the available resources while the robust watershed management programs currently underway will be instrumental in improving the state of the environment;
6. Agro-processing particularly food-processing will be one of the possible outcomes as increased agricultural production will attract private investors who anticipate opportunities for engaging in agro-processing and packaging of products;
7. Fishery could be one field of productive activity that could be boosted as a result of water development schemes thereby leading to improved livelihood of those to be engaged in the undertaking.
8. As large-scale farms are to engage in measures related to water and land development particularly in Upper and Lower Beles, there could be greater opportunity for gainful employment opportunities and mobility both within the project areas and beyond.
9. Since the area has a potential to enhance tourism, the development of tourist attraction sites and innovative enterprises could be translated into increased development of the regions in which projects are located.

Owing to these and other expected changes, it will be useful to monitor changes, assess the impact of development interventions, and document the kind of development activities that are realized. Such understanding will help not only efforts aimed at monitoring changes but also could be instrumental in identifying areas of possible policy inputs and improvements that could benefit from lived experiences with regard to launching other similar undertakings. It goes without saying that monitoring change and identifying experienced impacts necessitate conducting baseline studies that would facilitate efforts in making periodic assessments and evaluation of development interventions over time. In this vein, the proposed baseline study is hoped to produce a data base of situations characterizing the status quo thereby serving as a springboard for successive studies in terms of impact assessment. The focus will thus be on determining the situation of the local population and local economy from the point of view of food production, land tenure, food security, and poverty alleviation endeavors. The study is limited to the Tana sub-basin as the construction of the envisaged irrigation schemes is underway in the sub-basin.

1.2 Objectives

The overall objective of the study is aimed at generating a baseline data for monitoring the overall impact of development interventions in general and the irrigation schemes of the Tana sub-basin in particular regarding local livelihoods, food security and poverty alleviation in rural areas and local employment and income, assets and access to services in urban areas.

The specific objectives include:

1. Identifying the existing rural production system by focusing on crops and livestock production and marketing, land size holding and allocation system
2. Providing an overview of the rural livelihood system by identifying assets possession, housing and health status, and non-farm activities.
3. Identifying the existing employment types and business trends in urban centers;
4. Providing an overview of assets possession, expenditure patterns and linkages of urban households;
5. Identifying the health and housing status of urban households;
6. Identifying possible research questions that could further be taken up by the FSS in its engagement of socio-economic study of the area

1.3 Research Questions (issues)

In line with the aforementioned, the following major research questions (issues) will be posed and addressed in the course of conducting the study. In view of the fact that this study is mainly exploratory in nature and approach, the research questions will be formulated in view of the existing state of affairs on the ground as follows:

- What is the socio-economic profile (family size, age-sex structure, income, health and educational situation, access to services, migration/relocation… etc) of the study populations at the time of conducting this study?
- What are the major sources of livelihood, production systems, and life patterns of the study population?
- What does the poverty and food security situation prevalent in the area look like?
- What is the current situation regarding land tenure system in terms of security, access, average holding, and common property regime in the study areas?
- What are the existing patterns of urban development and rural-urban network in the study locations?

- What are the pros and cons of development interventions in the study area as perceived by the local people, government officials, and development partners?
- What are the major types of employment and work status of urban househ
- What does the income status of the urban households look like?
- What is the health and housing status of urban households?
- What are the expenditure and linkage patterns of urban households?
- What possible areas could be identified for further research and study?

1.4. Methodology

The following illustrates the sampling procedures, data to be collected and data collection techniques for rural and urban households.

1.4.1 *Sampling*

The location of the study in the Tana Sub-Basin has covered 5 *woredas* in the Amhara Regions. The study will use multistage sampling ranging from selection of *woredas* to households

- **Sampling the Study *Woredas and towns***

Owing to the vastness of the study area, it will be appropriate to sample *woredas* first stage. The *woredas,* which are the beneficiaries of the irrigation project selected purposively. Accordingly five *woredas,* namely Dembia, Fogera, Gondar Libokemekm and Mecha were selected. Each of these *woredas* is a beneficiary irrigation scheme. Dembia and Gondar zuria benefits from Megech irrigation p Fogera and Libokemkem benefit from Rib irrigation project and Mecha benefits Koga irrigation project (see figure 1).

With regard to the selection of towns, the capital city of each of the study wor chosen as the study town. Hence the selected towns are Qoladiba (Dembiya), Mak (Gondar Zuria), Addis Zemen (Libokemekem), Woreta (Fogera), Merawi (Mech addition Bahr Dar was also included as the study site since Bahr Dar is the major the surrounding and changes that might come in the surrounding areas could infl the livelihood households in Bahr Dar.

- **Sampling Rural and Urban *Kebeles***

The second stage in the sampling procedure relates to identifying rural and urban *kebeles*. Accordingly, two rural *kebeles* which are covered by the irrigation projects within each *woreda* are selected purposively in consultation with the *woreda* administration. A total of 10 rural kebeles were selected and these are shown in Table 1.3. With regard to urban kebeles, Accordingly one urban kebele was selected randomly in each city. In Bahr Dar city however two kebeles were selected randomly owing the size of the city. In general a total of seven kebeles were selected.

- **Sampling Households**

Households were randomly selected from each of the rural and urban study *kebeles* by making use of the lists of households obtained from *kebele* offices as sampling frame. A fixed size of fifty households were selected from each of the study *kebele* making the total sample size to be 500 rural households and 350 urban households. The use of fixed number of households is to avoid the problem that may arise if proportional sampling is used.

Table 1.3: Selected *woredas*, towns and rural and urban study *kebeles* and sample size

Irrigation scheme	Beneficary *woredas*	Rural Study *Kebeles*	Rural House hold sample size	Study town	Urban study ebele	Urban houshold sample size
Megech	Dembia	Guramba bota Sereba debel	50 50	Qoladeba	01	50
	Gondar zuria	Hamsafei Tach teda	50 50	Makesegint e	01	50
Rib	Libokemkem	Bambiko Shinatsion	50 50	Addis Zemen	02	50
	Fogera	Rib Gebriel Shaga	50 50	Woreta	01	50
Koga	Mecha	Amarit Kudamee	50 50	Merawe	03	50
				Bahirdar	Hidar 11 Sefersel am	50 50
Total	5	10	500	6		350

SOURCE: Filed Data

1.4.2 *Types of Data, Data collection techniques, and Data Sources*

- **Type of Data**

Collected data include those that help in understanding the research problem and addressing the research questions. The data are also limited to those critical ones in order to make the questionnaire manageable. With slight differences for rural and urban households, the collected data are the following:

1. Population characteristics

- Age-sex composition, ethnic and religious composition, educational level, primary activity;

2. Migration status

- Incidence;
- Reasons for migration;
- Duration of migration

3. Livelihood

- Agriculture/crops;
- Agriculture/livestock;
- Non-farm, migration, rural urban linkage

4.Housing and health

- Housing characteristics, such as building material for roofs, number of rooms, indoor, in door sanitary conditions, etc.
- Perception of health, recurrently occurring diseases and utilization of health care services

5. Food security

- Food status; food aid
- Months of food shortages

6.Assets

- Physical assets
- Financial assets

7. Access to services

- Access to health services;
- Access to education;
- Access to water supply;

8. Household income and expenditure

- Income source and amount;
- Household expenditure

9. Expectations from irrigation schemes

Data collection techniques

Structured interviews: The main instrument used in the study was structured questionnaires/interview guides dealing with livelihood and socio-economic situations of the study population.

In -depth interviews: Interviews were conducted with the relevant *woreda* and *kebele* officials, sector office heads and experts regarding the present state of infrastructure, development problems of the area, land tenure and the envisaged change in the study localities.

Desk review: secondary sources in the form of official policy documents, statistical reports containing baseline and current data, and available research reports relevant to the study theme were consulted.

Figure 1: Location map of the study *woredas* and irrigation schemes

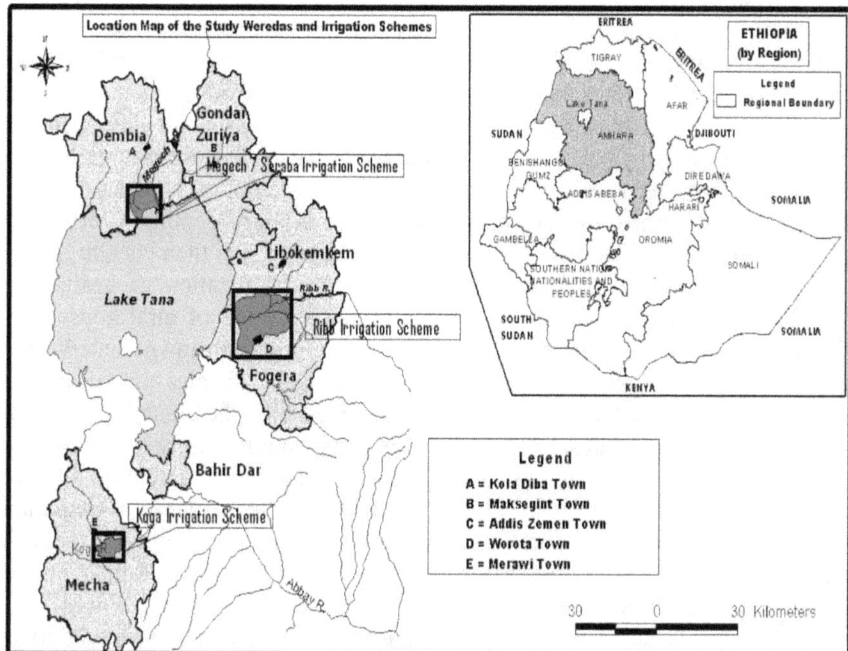

1.5 Significance and Policy Implications

It is hoped that once baseline data with regard to the existing situation is collected, it will serve as a basis for monitoring the changes through comparison of data to be gathered periodically (every other year). This could form the basis that would inform policy makers and practitioners in a manner that could enable them foresee implications accruing from subsequent developments and take appropriate measures in good time with a view to avert unintended outcomes and consequences that negatively impinge on the livelihood of the local people, the environment, and other concerns associated with realizing development goals and objectives.

1.6 Organization of the Report

Section one of this report is the introductory part in which the background, purposes and methodology are stated. The findings of the rural households are outlined between chapters two to chapter seven while the findings of the urban households are outlined between chapters eight to fourteen..

Chapter two deals with the population characteristics of the rural households. In this section, the report describes the age-sex composition, family size, headship, education, ethnic and religious characteristics and primary activities. Chapter three is a section on agriculture. This section is divided into crop and livestock production and illustrates patterns of land holding, crop production and livestock production. Chapter four identifies asset ownership of households. The section is divided into two: physical and financial assets. Chapter five focuses on housing and health characteristics of rural households. The section on housing discusses the housing structure, overcrowding and indoor sanitary conditions while the section on health discusses households' perception of their health status, recurrently occurring diseases, maternal death and utilization of health care services. Chapter six outlines the income and expenditure of rural households. Chapter seven is a section on households' interaction with town centers, their engagement in non-farm activities and their food status. Chapter eight deals with the population characteristics of the urban sampled households under study. In this section, the report describes the age-sex composition, family size, headship, education, ethnic and religious characteristics and primary activities. Chapter nine is a section on migration. This section discusses the incidence of migration, reasons for migration and duration of migration. Chapter ten outlines the main employment types in the study towns, incomes derived thereof and the nature of businesses in the study areas. Chapter eleven is about access to services while section twelve discusses the possession of assets by households. Section thirteen discusses the expenditure and linkage patters. Section fourteen is about food status, coping strategies and well being. Chapter fifteen suggests some possible researchable issues on the basis of the base line survey.

II. POPULATION CHARACTERISTICS OF RURAL HOUSEHOLDS

2.1. Age-Sex Composition

Table 2.1 shows that the total household members of the study sample are 2656. Male members of the total households form 1477 or 55.6 % while the female members form 1171 or 44.6%. Accordingly, the sex-ratio is 126.1 or there are 126 males for every 100 females.

Though all *woredas* have higher number of males than females, variation in sex ratio is noted among them. Mecha, with the smallest ratio, has 117 males for every 100 females while Fogera with 139 males for every 100 females has the highest number of males for females (Table 2.2). All other *woredas* lie between these two extremes.

The age structure is indicative of the fertility and mortality experience of a given population. Table 2.1 reveals that the age structure of the study population exhibits a situation of high fertility where a large proportion of the population belongs to the younger age group or below 15 years. Those below 15 years of age form 45.1% implying that a significant size of household members are youngsters who are not able to join the labor force. The sex distribution of this age group shows that males are 45.8% and females are 44.4%. On the other hand it is only 2.2 % of the household members who are above the age of 64. The age group which can join the labor force thus forms 52.7 % of the total population.

Table 2.1 Age sex distribution of total members of households

	Total		
Age group	M	F	T
0-4	10.8	9.5	10.2
5-9	16.9	18.8	17.7
10-14	18.1	16.1	17.2
15-19	13.7	10.2	12.2
20-24	6.9	5.3	6.2
25-29	3.9	6.7	5.1
30-34	2.9	6.9	4.7
35-39	5.2	10.4	7.5
40-44	5.7	6.1	5.9
45-49	5.3	4.4	4.9
50-54	3.9	2.0	3.0

55-59	2.3	1.0	1.7
60-64	1.6	1.1	1.4
65-69	0.9	0.4	0.7
70& over	1.9	1.0	1.5
N	1477	1178	2656
Sex ratio			126.1

SOURCE: filed Data

The age dependency ratio which is the ratio of non-productive persons (persons aged 0 to 14 and 65 and over) to persons aged 15 to 64 was estimated on the basis of a broader age group distribution (Table 2.3). Accordingly, the overall dependency ratio is 90% or 0.9 which implies that there is nearly one dependent person for every one actively working person. *Woreda* variation is noticeable in that the dependency ratio is higher in Libokemkem (97%) and Mecha (96%) compared to other *woredas*. The young dependency ratio is 86% while the old dependency ratio is 4.1%. This implies that the young dependents are significant for every working person.

Table 2.2 : Age sex distribution of households by *woreda*

	Dembia			Fogera			Gondar zuria			Libokemkem			Mecha		
Age group	M	F	T	M	F	T	M	F	T	M	F	T	M	F	T
0-4	16.4	10.4	13.8	11.8	5.0	9.0	6.4	10.7	8.3	12.0	14.1	13.0	7.1	7.1	7.1
5-9	15.1	18.9	16.7	19.4	17.8	18.7	14.5	17.7	16.0	19.0	18.3	18.7	16.3	20.9	18.4
10-14	13.8	13.5	13.7	15.8	16.4	16.2	19.9	15.6	18.0	16.5	15.8	16.2	24.4	19.0	21.9
15-19	11.7	8.6	10.4	14.5	9.1	12.2	15.9	11.5	13.9	12.7	10.8	11.8	13.9	10.7	12.4
20-24	8.7	5.0	7.1	5.6	7.3	6.3	6.8	6.2	6.5	6.3	5.4	5.9	7.1	2.8	5.1
25-29	3.7	11.3	6.9	4.6	6.8	5.5	4.4	4.1	4.3	4.2	7.1	5.5	2.4	4.7	3.5
30-34	5.7	7.7	6.5	3.0	6.8	4.6	2.0	5.3	3.5	2.5	7.9	5.0	1.4	6.7	3.8
35-39	4.7	10.4	7.1	2.3	9.6	5.3	5.7	10.3	7.8	8.8	9.5	9.1	4.7	12.3	8.2
40-44	7.0	4.5	6.0	5.3	7.3	6.1	5.4	7.0	6.1	4.2	5.0	4.6	6.4	6.7	6.6
45-49	3.4	4.5	3.8	4.3	5.5	4.8	6.8	4.9	5.9	4.9	2.5	3.8	7.5	4.7	6.2
50-54	2.7	1.8	2.3	4.3	3.2	3.8	4.7	2.1	3.5	3.9	2.1	3.0	3.7	1.2	2.6
55-59	2.3	0.9	1.7	2.6	1.8	2.3	3.0	0.0	1.7	1.8	0.8	1.3	1.7	1.6	1.6
60-64	2.0	1.8	1.9	3.0	0.5	1.9	0.7	2.1	1.3	1.1	0.4	0.8	1.4	0.8	1.1
65-69	1.0	0.0	0.6	1.3	0.9	1.1	1.0	0.8	0.9	0.7	0.4	0.6	0.7	0.0	0.4
70& over	1.7	0.9	1.3	2.3	1.8	2.1	2.7	1.6	2.2	1.4	0.0	0.8	1.4	0.8	1.1
N	298	222	520	304	219	524	296	243	539	284	241	525	295	253	548
Sex ratio			134.2			138.8			121.8			117.8			116.6

SOURCE: filed data

Table 2.3: Percentage distribution of population by broader age group and dependency ratio

	Age group			Dependency ratio		
	<15	15-64	65 & over	Young	Old	Total
Dembia	44.2	53.9	1.9	82.0	3.5	85.5
Fogera	43.9	52.9	3.2	83.0	6.0	89.0
Gondar Zurai	42.3	54.6	3.1	77.5	5.6	83.1
Libokemek	47.9	50.7	1.4	94.5	2.7	97.2
Mecha	47.4	51.1	1.5	92.7	2.9	95.6
Total	45.1	52.7	2.2	85.6	4.1	89.7

SOURCE: filed data

2.2 Household Composition and Marital Status

In terms of household composition, household headship and size matters. Headship has an important socio-economic significance. For instance, female-headed households provide pertinent information for gender oriented interventions. In the same way, household size affects the socio-economic well being of household members.

As presented in Table 2.4, the vast majority of households (94%) in the study area are male-headed households, while 6 % of the households are female-headed. *Woreda* variation is insignificant in this case. The Table reveals that there are on average about 5 persons in each household. The household size however varies from a single person (0.8%) to more than seven persons (32%). In some *woredas*, such as Gondar zuria (43%), Mecha (37%) households with seven and more than seven members are significant.

Table 2.4: Percentage distribution of households by sex of household head, household size and place of residence

Characteristics	Dembia	Fogera	Gondar Zuria	Libokemkem	Mecha	Total
Household headship						
Male	92.0	95.0	98.0	94.0	91.0	94.0
Female	8.0	5.0	2.0	6.0	9.0	6.0
Number of usual household members						
1	0.0	0.0	2.0	1.0	1.0	0.8
2	5.0	6.0	6.0	7.0	6.0	6.0
3	10.0	9.0	9.0	7.0	4.0	7.8
4	14.0	16.0	8.0	18.0	12.0	13.6
5	28.0	25.0	18.0	15.0	15.0	20.2
6	18.0	16.0	14.0	24.0	25.0	19.4
7 or more	25.0	28.0	43.0	28.0	37.0	32.2
Average household size	5.19	5.20	5.48	5.23	5.57	5.33

SOURCE: filed data

The marital status of household reveals that the overwhelming majority (95%) are married. Those who have ceased to live in union are very few. It is only 2.4% and 0.2 % who are divorced and separated respectively. Those who are divorced are slightly higher in Mecha (6%).

Table 2.5: Marital status of household heads

Woreda	Single	Married	Divorced	Separated
Dembia	0.0	97.0	2.0	1.0
Fogera	1.0	97.9	0.0	0.0
Gondar zuria	1.0	98.0	1.0	0.0
Libokemkem	0.0	97.0	3.0	0.0
Mecha	3.0	91.0	6.0	0.0
Total	1.0	95.2	2.4	0.2

SOURCE: filed data

2.3 Ethnic and Religious Composition

Almost all household heads in the study area belong to the Amhara ethnic group and are also orthodox Christians (Table 2.6). There is therefore less diversity both in terms of ethnicity and religious beliefs in the study *woredas*.

Table 2.6: Percentage distribution of household head by ethnic group and religion

Woreda	Ethnic group		Religion	
	Amhara	Others[1]	Orthodox Christians	Muslims
Dembia	99.0	1.0	100.0	0.0
Fogera	99.0	1.0	100.0	0.0
Gondar zuria	100.0	0.0	100.0	0.0
Libokemekem	99.0	1.0	100.0	0.0
Mecha	97.9	2.0	99.0	1.0
Total	99.0	1.0	99.8	0.2

SOURCE: filed data

2.4 Educational Characteristics

Table 2.7, which reveals the educational status of respondents, shows that a substantial proportion of the population (48%) aged 6 years and over is illiterate. The illiterates are much higher in Dembia (57%) and Fogera (54%). With such substantial proportion of the population being illiterate, the society is not benefiting from the positive benefits of education.

[1] In the other category, there were 4 persons who reported Oromo ethnicity and one person who reported Tigray ethnicity

Table 2.7: Percentage distribution of respondents aged 6 years and over by Educational status.

Woreda	Dembia	Fogera	Gondar zuria	Libokemekem	Mecha	Total
None	57.3	53.6	44.0	49.5	38.8	48.3
Read only	2.8	0.9	1.7	4.4	0.8	2.0
Read and write only	13.7	43.3	22.4	6.0	8.9	18.9
Kindergarten	0.0	0.0	0.4	0.0	0.4	0.2
Primary	18.6	1.8	21.2	33.9	40.0	23.3
Junior Secondary	5.8	0.0	3.9	4.8	7.1	4.4
Secondary	1.6	0.4	6.4	1.4	3.7	2.8
Diploma	0.2	0.0	0.0	0.0	0.2	0.1
N	431	453	482	436	492	2294

SOURCE: filed data

The disaggregation of respondents by sex shows that there are more illiterate females (58%) than males (41%) (Table 2.8). With regard to formal education, a significant proportion (23%) are in primary school with Libokemekme (34%) and Mecha (40%) having a higher proportion of the population who are attending primary school. There are more males (25.4%) than females (21%) who are attending primary schools. Those in the junior and senior secondary schools are only 7.2% with males in this category forming 7.3% and females being 6.8%.

Table 2.8 Percentage distribution of respondents aged 6 years and over by Educational status and sex.

Woreda	Dembia		Fogera		Gondar Zuria		Libokemkeem		Mecha		Total	
	M	F	M	F	M	F	M	F	M	F	M	F
None	50.4	66.3	46.6	62.8	36.5	53.6	41.6	59.1	29.9	49.6	40.7	57.9
Read only	2.5	3.2	0.8	1.0	2.2	0.9	4.6	4.0	1.5	0.0	2.3	1.8
Read and write only	19.7	5.9	49.9	34.7	28.4	14.7	8.4	3.0	13.4	3.6	24.1	12.3
Kindergarten	0.0	0.0	0.0	0.0	0.7	0.0	0.0	0.0	0.0	0.9	0.2	0.2
Primary	19.3	17.6	2.0	1.5	22.5	19.4	38.2	28.8	44.4	34.8	25.4	20.8
Junior Secondary	7.4	3.7	0.0	0.0	3.3	4.7	5.9	3.5	6.7	7.6	4.6	4.0
Secondary	0.8	2.7	0.8	0.0	6.3	6.6	1.3	1.5	4.1	3.1	2.7	2.8
Diploma	0.0	0.5	0.0	0.0	0.0	0.0	0.0	0.0	0.0	0.4	0.0	0.2
N	244	187	253	199	271	211	238	198	268	224	1274	1019

SOURCE: filed data

2.5 Primary Activity

Table 2.9 shows that 40% of the total population aged 7 years and over are farmers, 35% are students and 11% classify themselves as home makers. Engagement in other activities, such as in private sector, government or parastatal and self employment as primary activity, is negligible. Farming is therefore the primary activity generating income in the study area. The disaggregation of primary activity by gender shows that 49% of males are farmers while females who classified themselves as farmers are 29%. A significant proportion (24%) of females classify themselves as home makers though in some *woredas* such as in Dembia (51%), Mecha (39%) the proportion of homer makers is higher. Since farming is a primary activity of the study population, any intervention to improve peoples's livelihood should focus on how to improve the farming activity.

Table 2.9: Percentage distribution of respondents aged 7 years and over by primary activity

		Dembia	Fogera	Gondar Zurai	Liboke mekem	Mecha	Total
Child	Male	14.5	15.6	10.9	11.7	14.2	13.4
	Female	13.2	12.1	8.3	8.1	12.8	10.9
	Total	13.9	14.1	9.8	10.1	13.6	12.3
Student	Male	27.2	32.9	41.9	34.2	42.5	36.0
	Female	25.8	27.4	38.2	36.8	41.3	34.2
	Total	26.6	30.6	40.3	35.3	41.9	35.2
home maker	Male	0.0	0.0	0.0	0.0	0.0	0.0
	Female	50.5	2.6	23.5	3.8	38.5	24.1
	Total	23.0	1.6	10.2	1.7	18.0	11.0
Government parastatal	Male	0.0	0.0	0.0	0.0	0.0	0.0
	Female	0.5	0.5	0.5	0.0	0.9	0.5
	Total	0.2	0.2	0.2	0.0	0.4	0.2
Private sector	Male	0.0	0.0	0.0	0.4	1.2	0.3
	Female	0.0	0.0	0.0	0.0	0.5	0.1
	Total	0.0	0.0	0.0	0.2	0.8	0.2

Self employed	Male	1.3	0.4	0.0	0.0	0.4	0.4
	Female	0.5	0.0	0.0	0.0	0.0	0.1
	Total	1.0	0.2	0.0	0.0	0.2	0.3
Farmer	Male	54.5	49.4	46.0	53.7	40.9	48.7
	Female	8.8	55.8	28.4	50.8	5.0	29.1
	Total	34.5	52.1	38.4	52.4	24.4	40.0
N	Male	235	243	265	231	254	1228
	Female	182	190	204	185	215	979
	Total	417	434	49	416	472	2208

SOURCE: filed data

III. AGRICULTURE

3.1 Crop Production

3.1.1 *Land Ownership*

The study has made enquiry regarding respondents' ownership of land in the five study *woredas*. As indicated in the following Table (3.1), the majority comprising 65% of the respondents within the age range of 31 and 50 years in Mecha *woreda* possess farmland on which they eke out their livelihood. This is followed in descending order of ownership by respondents in the same age group in Libo Kemkem (64%), Dembiya (62%), Gondar Zuria (59%), and Fogera (49%).

Table 3.1: Percentage of respondents owning land by age group, frequency and study *woreda*

Age group	*Woreda*					
	Fogera (%)	Gondar Zuria (%)	Dembiya (%)	Libo (%)	Mecha (%)	Total (Frequency)
21-30	13	9	8	15	8	53
31-40	20	22	32	37	23	134
41-50	29	37	30	27	42	165
51-60	17	19	18	15	18	87
61-70	14	6	8	2	5	35
71-80	5	4	3	4	4	20
81+	2	3	1	-	-	6
Total	**100**	**100**	**100**	**100**	**100**	**500**

SOURCE: Field Data

On the other hand, it was reported that respondents between the age range of 51 and 70 also own farm plots in all the study *woredas* in the following order: Fogera (31%), Dembiya (26%), Gondar Zuria (25%), Mecha (23%), and Libo (17%). As regards those within the age range of 21 and 30, the highest is recorded in Libo (15%), followed by Fogera (13%), Gondar Zuria (9%), and the two remaining *woredas*, namely Dembiya and Mecha (8% each), which is indicative of high incidence of landlessness affecting the youth in all the study locations. This implies that there is a need for those within this age group to look for other sources of livelihood in the face of the inevitable growing paucity of farm plots that could be put to use by young males and females in the years to come. Equally disconcerting is the situation of the aged falling under the category of the age group of over 71 years where only 7% possess own plots in Fogera and Gondar Zuria, 4% in Dembiya and none in Libo and Mecha. In the light of this, the likelihood of sustenance of the aged would thus depend on support by relatives and community associations and/or inclusion in safety net programs.

3.1.2 Number of Plots Owned and Average Distance Traveled to Farm Plots

Respondents in all the study *woredas* who own land were asked to provide information on the number of plots they own. This is provided in Table 3.2.

Table 3.2: Percentage of Respondents in Study *Woredas* by Number of Plots owned and Frequency in the study *woredas*

No. of Plots	***Woreda***					
	Fogera (%)	**Gondar Zuria (%)**	**Dembiya (%)**	**Libo (%)**	**Mecha (%)**	**Total (frequency)**
1	2	10	13	1	12	38
2	9	40	18	16	25	108
3	20	21	32	32	30	135
4	48	20	27	34	18	147
5	12	9	7	10	6	44
6	3	0	2	3	7	15
7	3	0	0	4	2	9
8	1	0	1	0	0	2
Total	**98**	**100**	**100**	**100**	**100**	**498**

SOURCE: field data

Information elicited from respondents in the study *woredas* indicate that the majority own between 3 and 5 plots in the following order: Fogera (80%), Libo (76%), Dembiya (66%), Mecha (54%), and Gondar Zuria (50%). Regarding those who possess between 1 and 2 plots is reported in Gondar Zuria (50%) followed by respondents from Mecha (37%), Dembiya (31%), Libo (17%), and Fogera (11%). The percentage of respondents who claimed owning between six and eight plots is negligible the highest being reported by informants from

Mecha and Dembiya (9%), and Libo (7% each), followed by 3% of the respondents in Dembiya and none in Gondar Zuria.

The average distance between the residences and farm plots of respondents in terms of km and time traveled by respondents vary between a minimum of 0.2 km (0.10 hr) and a maximum of 2.1 km (2hrs) as illustrated in Table 3.3.

Table 3.3 Average distance in hours and km traveled by respondents by study *woreda*

Woreda	Average distance in Km	Average distance in hr
Libo	0.2Km	0.10hr
Fogera	0.5Km	0.15hr
Gondar Z	0.5Km	0.15hr
Dembiya	1 km	0.30hr
Mecha	2.1Km	2.00hr

SOURCE: Field Data

3.1.3 *Size of Holding (ha)*

The baseline study has uncovered that a total of 663.5 ha of land is held by the 500 respondents in the five study *woredas*, which amounts to an average of over 1.3 ha/hh that is significant in view of per capita holding in the highlands of Ethiopia that is fairly below 1 hectare per family. Of these, the highest is recorded in Gondar Zuria (147 ha), followed by Dembiya (146ha), Fogera (135 ha), Mecha (131 ha), and Libo (106 ha) (Table 3.4).

Table 3.4: Total area of land holding of respondents by study *woreda*

Woreda	Total holding (ha)	Per capita holding
Fogera	135.108	1.35
Gondar Z	146.613	1.47
Dembiya	145.5	1.46
Libo	105.585	1.1
Mecha	130.6475	1.31
Total	**663.4535**	**1.3**

SOURCE: Field Data

Taken individually, the figures on average per capita land holding vary slightly in Fogera (1.35ha), Gondar Zuria (1.47ha), Dembiya (1.46ha), Libo (1.1ha), and Mecha (1.31ha).

3.1.4 *Other Forms of Land Holding by Respondents in the Selected Woredas*

Respondents were asked to provide information on other forms of land they plough in addition to what they own through renting, sharecropping, gift from relatives or other persons.

Table 3.5: Frequency of respondents renting land (ha) by *woreda*

Woreda	Frequency	Ha
Fogera	14	5.475
Gondar Z	39	47.38
Dembiya	28	105.25
Libo	38	19
Mecha	39	22.818
Total	**158**	**199.923 ha**

SOURCE: Field Data

In the five *woredas covered in the study*, it was reported that 158 respondents (31.6% of the total sample population) rent nearly 200 ha of land from others due to a variety of reasons associated with need and capacity. This brings the figure of the average per capita holding of rented land used by those concerned to 1.47 ha. As illustrated by the figures in Table 5.1, significant variations in terms of the size of rented land is observed across the *woredas* where the highest is recorded in Dembiya (105ha) and the lowest in Fogera (5.5 ha).

According to the data regarding the number and percentage of respondents that make use of land through other arrangements, it was reported that a total of 127 (25.4% of the total sample population) in all the *woredas* engage in sharecropping by accessing 84 ha of land for various agricultural activities. Here too, variation across the locations studied is observed whereby the highest in terms of size of land acquired through sharecropping is recorded in Dembiya (53 ha) and the lowest in Mecha (slightly over 2 ha).

In the same vein, attempt is made to elicit information as regards the number of people in the five selected *woredas* who obtained land through gifs, which is negligible in terms of the number of beneficiaries and the size of land acquired.

Table 3.6: Percentage and frequency of respondents who engage in sharecropping by land size (ha) and *woreda*

Woreda	Percentage and Frequency	Land (ha)
Fogera	23 (%)	8.025
Gondar Z	23 (%)	19.125
Dembiya	63 (%)	53.125
Libo	3 (%)	1.375
Mecha	15 (%)	2.25
Total	**127 (frequency)**	**83.9 ha**

SOURCE: Field Data

As shown in the Table, only 32 respondents (6.4% of the sample population) benefited in obtaining less than 9 ha of land through gifts with minor variations across the locations studied.

Table 3.7: Percentage and frequency of respondents who obtained land through gift by land size and study *woreda*

Woreda	Percentage and Frequency	Land Size (ha)
Fogera	8	2.4
Gondar Z	2	0.5
Dembiya	1	2
Libo	6	1.875
Mecha	15	2
Total	**32**	**8.75**

SOURCE: Field Data

3.1.5 Possession of Private Fallow and Grazing Land

Informants were asked whether they possess private fallow and grazing land during the 2004 E.C production year. The data elicited in this regard is presented in Table 3.8. Accordingly, during the year in question only 15 respondents (3% of the total sample population) reported to have fallow land whereas the number of those who claimed to possess private grazing land during the same period is 86 (17.2 % of the total sample population).

Table 3.8: Percentage of respondents owning fallow and private grazing land by *woreda* in 2004 EC

Woreda	Own Fallow Land (frequency)	% of *woreda* Sample	Own Grazing Land (frequency)	% of *woreda* sample
Fogera	1	1	37	37
Gondar Z	1	1	14	14
Dembiya	2	2	5	5
Libo	6	6	17	17
Mecha	5	5	58	58
Total	**15**	**3%**	**86**	**17.2%**

SOURCE: Field Data

As indicated in the figures in the Table, the number of sample households who own fallow land is highly negligible in terms of frequency and percentage of respondents computed both at the level of the *woreda* sample populations and overall study sample. On the other hand, the highest number and percentage of ownership of private grazing land at the level of the sample population in the *woredas* covered in the study is recorded in Mecha (58%) while the lowest is registered in Dembiya (5%).

3.1.6 Land Use Certification and Security of Tenure

Of the total number of respondents constituting the sample populations in the *woredas*, 447 (89.4%) reported that they had obtained land certificates. Those who feel that they enjoy security of tenure are a bit more numbering 468 (93.6%).

Table 3.9 Frequency and Percentage of Respondents Who Received Land Certificates and Claiming to Enjoy Tenure Security

Woreda	Received Land Certificate	% of *woreda* Sample	Enjoy Tenure Security	% of *woreda* Sample
Fogera	83	83	93	93
Gondar Z	91	91	96	96
Dembiya	92	92	92	92
Libo	96	96	92	92
Mecha	85	85	95	95
Total	**447**	89.4	**468**	**93.6**

SOURCE: Field Data

3.1.7 *Possession of Plough Oxen*

It was established that 446 out of a total of the 500 respondents (89.2%) own plough oxen that are used for farming activities. As indicated in Table 3.10, per capita ownership of oxen in the sampled *woredas* is less than 2 per household. This implies that there is a need to pair oxen on the part of two or more households to engage in farming through collaborative arrangements.

Table 3.10: Frequency and percentage of respondents who own oxen by mean ownership and *woredas*

Woreda	Frequency and Percentage	Mean
Fogera	73 (%)	1.82
Gondar Z	95 (%)	1.66
Dembiya	93 (%)	1.68
Libo	94 (%)	1.77
Mecha	91 (%)	1.87
Total	**446 (frequency)**	**1.76 (total)**

SOURCE: Field Data

It could be observed from the foregoing that 54 (nearly 11%) of the farming households in the sample population surveyed in all the *woredas* do not own oxen implying that they have to resort to other means for ploughing their plots. The highest incidence of paucity in this regard is recorded in Fogera where 27% of the respondents do not have oxen whereas in the remaining 4, the situation ranges between 9% in Mecha and 5% in Gondar Zuria.

3.1.8 *Usage of Farm Implements*

Attempt was also made to identify the means like iron and/or wood implements for farming purposes. It was learnt that the frequency and percentage of respondents using these implements is higher in Gondar Zuria (15%) followed by those in Fogera and Mecha (13% each), and Dembiya and Libo where 8% and 7% are recorded respectively.

Table 3.11 Percentage of respondents using simple iron and wood implements for farming by age group and sample woreda

	Woreda				
Age group	**Fogera %**	**Gondar Zuria. %**	**Dembiya %**	**Libo %**	**Mecha %**
21-30	4	4	0	0	0
31-40	0	4	2	3	3
41-50	2	2	2	2	3
51-60	4	0	2	2	4
61-70	0	0	2	0	3
71-80	3	1	0	0	0
81+	0	4	0	0	0
Total %	**13**	**15**	**8**	**7**	**13**

SOURCE: Field Data

3.1.9. *Means and Ways of Engaging in Farming Activities*

Respondents in the sample *woredas* were asked to identify the means they employ for engaging in farming activities by identifying whether this was done through exchanging labor for oxen, leasing land to make use of oxen owned by others, and using traditional mutual self-help associations like *debo* and *w/senfel.*

By and large, the percentage of respondents who exchange labor for oxen as means of engaging in farming is negligible in all the study *woredas*. As indicated in Table 3.12, only 3% of the respondents in Dembiya, Libo and Mecha resort to this practice whereas none was reported as regards Gondar Zuria.

Table 3.12: Percentage of respondents exchanging labor for oxen by age group and study woreda

	Woreda				
Age group	**Fogera**	**Gondar Z**	**Dembiya**	**Libo**	**Mecha**
21-30	0	0	0	0	0
31-40	1	0	1	0	1
41-50	0	0	0	0	1
51-60	0	0	0	0	0
61-70	0	0	1	0	1
71-80	1	0	1	0	0
81+	0	0	0	0	0
Total %	**2**	**0**	**3**	**3**	**3**

SOURCE: Field Data

The practice of leasing land to those who own oxen for farming purposes is also similarly negligible across all the locations covered in this study as indicated in Table 3.13.

Table 3.13: Percentage of respondents who lease land to those with oxen by age group and study woreda

	Woreda				
Age group	**Fogera**	**Gondar Z**	**Dembiya**	**Libo**	**Mecha**
21-30	0	0	0	0	0
31-40	1	0	1	0	0
41-50	0	1	0	0	1
51-60	0	0	0	0	0
61-70	0	0	1	0	1
71-80	1	0	1	0	0
81+	0	0	0	0	0
Total %	**2**	**1**	**3**	**0**	**2**

SOURCE: Field Data

As observed in Table 3.14, the percentage of respondents who affirmed that they engage in farming through using own labor ranges from as high as 12% in Fogera to 9% in Gondar Zuria and Libo whereas Mecha and Dembiya registered intermediate ranges of 11% and 10% respectively.

Table 3.14: Percentage of respondents who engage in farming through own labor by age group and sample *woreda*.

	Woreda				
Age group	**Fogera**	**Gondar Zuria**	**Dembiya**	**Libo**	**Mecha**
21-30	2	1	2	2	2
31-40	2	2	2	2	2
41-50	2	2	1	2	2
51-60	2	1	1	1	2
61-70	1	1	2	1	2
71-80	1	1	1	1	1
81+	2	1	1	0	0
Total %	**12**	**9**	**10**	**9**	**11**

SOURCE: Field Data

In sharp contrast to the aforementioned, use of hired labor appears to be widely practiced by high percentage of respondents in all the *woredas* as illustrated in Table 3.15. In the woredas covered by the study, the phenomenon of using hired labor in farming activities ranges from a minimum of 93% in Mecha to as high as 100% in Libo. One explanatory factor for this could be the high incidence of landlessness that is believed to be prevalent in the study locations.

Table 3.15: Percentage of respondents who engage in farming by using hired labor by age group and *woreda*

	Woreda				
Age group	**Fogera**	**Gondar Z**	**Dembiya**	**Libo**	**Mecha**
21-30	13	9	8	15	5
31-40	19	21	32	37	22
41-50	29	37	29	27	40
51-60	16	19	17	15	18
61-70	14	6	8	2	4
71-80	5	4	3	4	4
81+	1	1	1	0	0
Total %	**97**	**97**	**98**	**100**	**93**

SOURCE: Field Data

It also appears that taking recourse to traditional mutual self-help associations *(debo, wenfel)* through which communities pool their labor and farm oxen/tools together for farming activities is fairly practiced in the areas covered in the study as illustrated in Table s 3.16 and 3.17.

Table 3.16: Percentage of respondents who engage in farming by using *debo* by age group and sample *woreda*

	Woreda				
Age group	**Fogera**	**Gondar Zuria**	**Dembiya**	**Libo**	**Mecha**
21-30	2	8	0	1	0
31-40	2	24	32	2	0
41-50	0	21	29	0	3
51-60	0	15	17	0	0
61-70	0	6	8	0	0
71-80	0	2	3	0	0
81+	0	1	1	0	0
Total %	**4**	**77**	**90**	**3**	**3**

SOURCE: Field Data

Variations in terms of using *debo* among the *woredas* is significant ranging between as low as 3% in Libo and Mecha to as high as 77% and 90% in Gondar Zuria and Dembiya respectively. This might be an indication of variability in terms of the degree of the entrenchment of mutual self-help associational life in the culture of the communities in the different locations.

Table 3.17: Percentage of respondents who engage in farming by using w*enfel by* age group and sample *woreda*

	Woreda				
Age group	**Fogera**	**Gondar Z**	**Dembiya**	**Libo**	**Mecha**
21-30	3	0	1	7	0
31-40	2	8	1	18	0
41-50	2	8	3	22	3
51-60	0	7	4	12	0
61-70	1	1	1	4	0
71-80	0	2	1	3	0
81+	0	1	0	0	0
Total %	**8**	**27**	**11**	**66**	**3**

SOURCE: Field Data

In the same manner as in the case of the former, the use of the latter is by variations in terms of occurrence ranging from as low as 3% in Mecha to as high as 66% in Libo presumably for the same reasons indicated earlier.

3.1.10. *Annual Production (Base Year 2004 EC)*

Production data were elicited from respondents indicating the amount produced per hectare during the spring (*belg*) and major harvest seasons (*meher*) last year.

As observed in Table 3.18, mean annual production was 6.7 quintals/ha and 28.3 quintals/ha for all the *woredas* covered in the study during the spring and major harvest seasons respectively. In the former case, average production ranged from as low as 2 quintals/ha in Dembiya to as high as 10.8 quintals/ha in Fogera whereas in the latter case this was between 17.4 quintals/ha in Gondar Zuria and 44.7 quintals/ha in Libo. It could thus be assumed that the variability in the volume of production is influenced by several factors like availability of rainfall, soil fertility, and the degree and extent of applying improved inputs like quality seed, pesticide, and fertilizer, among others.

Table 3.18: Average crop production in 2004 EC during *belg* and *meher* seasons per ha in 2004 EC by sample *woreda*

Woreda	Av. *belg* production/ha (quintals)	Av. *meher* production (quintals)
Fogera	10.83	30.2625
Gondar Zuria	3.66	17.426
Dembiya	2	26.66198
Libo	7.99	44.65
Mecha	9.09	22.42
Average	**6.71**	**28.3**

SOURCE: Field Data

3.1.11 *Use of Agricultural Inputs*

Respondents in the selected *woredas* were asked whether they make use of agricultural inputs like chemical fertilizers, manure, improved seeds, and pesticides and herbicides on their plots for ensuring agricultural productivity (Table 3.19).

Table 3.19: Percentage of respondents using different agricultural inputs on their farms by *woreda*

Woreda	**chemical fertilizer (%)**	**Manure (%)**	**improved seeds (%)**	**Pesticides (%)**	**Herbicide (%)**
Fogera	54	46	14	74	32
Gondar Z	90	73	59	49	25
Dembiya	53	63	59	91	13
Libo	38	7	4	87	23
Mecha	99	99	100	39	39
Mean (%)	**66.8**	**57.6**	**47.2**	**68**	**26.4**

SOURCE: Field Data

The data on the use of agricultural inputs in the *woredas surveyed in the study* indicate that an average of 68% of the sample population reported that pesticides are used on their farms for boosting land productivity. This is followed by application of chemical fertilizers (66.8%), manure (57.6%), and improved seeds (47.2%).

Table 3.20 sheds light on the percentage of respondents using agricultural inputs during various farming seasons in the selected *woredas* as provided below.

Table 3.20: Percentage of respondents using inputs during various farming seasons by *woreda*

Woreda	**% *meher***	**% *belg***	% both *meher* and *belg*
Fogera	13	1	1
Gondar Z	60	0	1
Dembiya	59	0	0
Libo	3	1	0
Mecha	100	0	0

SOURCE: Field Data

As indicated above, the majority of respondents in the *woredas covered by the study* largely use inputs during the major harvest season, namely *meher* rather than during *belg at* the time of the coming of small rains.

The study has also endeavored to identify the reasons for not using improved agricultural inputs as reported by several informants in the different locations (Table 3.21). As shown in the Table, the majority of respondents numbering 294 (59%) attributed the reason for not using inputs to absence of need. Of these 96%, 71%, 52%, 43%, and 32% were from Libo, Gondar Zuria, Dembiya, Fogera and Mecha respectively. This is followed by scarcity of inputs as indicated by 71 informants (14.2%) of the total sample population).

Table 3.21: Percentage of respondents who do not use improved inputs and reasons for not using by *woreda*

Reasons	Fogera	Gondar Zuria	Dembiya	Libo	Mecha	Total
High cost of inputs	18	3	8	13	4	46
Unavailability	3	15	45	0	12	75
Lack of familiarity in using	16	7	2	11	1	37
Absence of need for using	43	71	52	96	32	294
Poor distribution of inputs	0	0	0	0	0	0
Land given out for sharecropping	0	1	0	1	0	2
Unfavorable landscape	0	1	0	1	0	2
Unsuitable weather condition	0	0	0	0	0	0
Belief that it attracts pests	15	2	1	0	0	18
Preference for local seed	0	0	0	0	0	0
No many cattle producing dung	15	2	1	0	0	18
Use of dung for fuel	0	2	28	0	1	31
Difficulty in transporting dung to farms	11	5	0	1	0	17
Other unspecified reasons	10	2	1	4	0	17

SOURCE: Field Data

Respondents provided information regarding the use of fertilizer by specifying the type of crop on which it is applied (Table 3.22). Accordingly, it was reported that of all the crops listed in the Table, *teff* is the one on which fertilizer is mostly applied both at the level of each sample *woreda* and all the locations covered by the study. This is followed by maize and wheat in descending order of frequency. With the exception of some crop types on which fertilizer is not applied in some *woredas*, it could be said that this input is applied on all types of crops with varying degree of intensity.

Table 3.22: Percentage of respondents who used fertilizer by crop type and *woreda*

crop type	Fogera	Gondar Zuria	Dembiya	Libo	Mecha	Total
Teff	34	82	42	0	65	223
Barley	3	4	6	1	81	95
Maize	7	44	41	1	98	191
Wheat	10	19	4	0	78	111
Sorghum	13	6	2	0	25	46
Sinar	9	0	2	0	0	11
Other cereals	3	1	0	1	12	17
Pulses	7	1	1	1	27	37
Oil seeds	10	0	0	0	15	25
Other	13	25	2	38	16	94

SOURCE: Field Data

Responses regarding the query on usage of improved seeds on different types of crops are provided in Table 3.23. Accordingly, maize and barley are identified as the type of crops on which improved seed is applied in descending order of frequency whereas the situation pertaining to other crops was found to be negligible in almost all cases. This could be due to a variety of reasons like shortage in supply, poor access and preference for locally produced varieties, among others.

Table 3.23: Percentage of respondents who used improved seeds by crop type and *woreda*

crop type	Fogera	Gondar Z	Dembiya	Libo	Mecha
Teff	1	9	1	0	1
Barley	0	0	1	0	1
Maize	2	39	48	0	96
Wheat	4	12	5	0	35
Sorghum	0	0	2	0	0
Sinar	1	0	0	0	0
Other cereals	2	0	0	0	0
Pulse	3	0	0	0	1
Oil seed	2	0	0	1	0
Other	4	0	3	3	0

SOURCE: Field Data

Informants were asked to provide information whether they obtained loans for purchasing inputs and the response to this query is indicated in Table 3.24. It was learnt that the average percentage of farmers who received loans for the stated purpose in the sample *woredas* is 21.2% the highest being in Gondar Zuria (53%) followed by Fogera (20%), Mecha (13%), Dembiya (12%), and Libo (8%).

Table 3.24: Percentage of respondents who received fertilizer loans by *woreda*

Woreda	%
Fogera	20
Gondar Zuria	53
Dembiya	12
Libo	8
Mecha	13
Mean	**21.2**

SOURCE: Field Data

In comparison, the average percentage of responses regarding seed loans is highly negligible amounting to only an average of 3% for all the locations.

Table 3.25: Percentage of respondents who took seed loans by *woreda*

Woreda	%
Fogera	2
Gondar Zuria	8
Dembiya	0
Libo	0
Mecha	5
Mean	**3**

SOURCE: Field Data

3.1.12. *Irrigated Agriculture*

In examining the engagement of the sample population in agricultural production, a query on whether farming households undertake irrigation for production purposes was posed. Based on the responses of informants in the sample *woredas*, Table 3.26 sheds light on the frequency and percentage of those who practice irrigation to this end.

Table 3.26: Frequency and percentage of respondents engaged in irrigated agriculture by *woreda*

Woreda	**Frequency and percentage**
Fogera	61
Gondar Zuria	62
Dembiya	100
Libo	71
Mecha	100
Mean	**78.8%**

SOURCE: Field Data

An average of nearly 79% of the sample population in the five *woredas* studied affirmed that they undertake irrigated agriculture of one kind or another. In the different *woredas*, variations in the frequency and percentage of the respondents who claim to have resorted to the practice is observed. Accordingly, whereas all respondents in Dembiya and Mecha reported that they engage in irrigated agricultural production as compared to those from Fogera and Gondar Zuria, where the practice is relatively less recorded as 61% and 62% respectively. One possible explanation for the high occurrence of engaging in irrigation in the case of the former two *woredas* could be the existence of government-led large scale irrigation schemes in the localities.

The study has also attempted to specifically identify the types of irrigated agriculture that are made use of by the farming households in the locations studied (Table 3.27).

Table 3.27: Frequency and percentage of respondents using different irrigation practices in the sample *woredas*

Woreda	Hand watering (%)	Flood diversion (%)	Furrow (%)	Use of Water retreat (%)	Other (%)
Fogera	3	1	33	5	18
Gondar Zuria	3	14	32	0	13
Dembiya	4	1	1	1	92
Libo	0	5	58	0	8
Mecha	2	0	96	0	0
Mean (%)	**3**	**4.2**	**44**	**1.2**	**26.2**

SOURCE: Field Data

In spite of significant claims of engaging in irrigated agricultural practices as indicated in Table 3.26, data on the frequency and percentage of use of different types of irrigation is relatively limited. As illustrated by the figures in Table 3.27, use of furrows or gullies by an average of 44% of the respondents in the study locations is highly pronounced. This is followed by an average of over 26% of the informants that claimed to have made use of other types, albeit without specifying what these are. The figures in Table 3.27 indicate that Dembiya (in terms of use of hand watering and other types) Gondar Zuria (in terms of use of flood diversion), Mecha (in terms of use of furrows), and Fogera (in terms of use of water retreat) registered high incidences of irrigated agricultural practices.

An attempt is also made to specify the use of other sources like dams, rivers, wells, streams and springs by the sample population in their practice of irrigated agriculture (Table 3.28).

Table 3.28: Frequency and percentage of respondents using other sources for irrigated agriculture by *woreda*

Woreda	Dams (%)	Rivers (%)	Wells (%)	Streams (%)	Springs (%)
Fogera	7	45	1	1	5
Gondar Zuria	0	62	0	0	0
Dembiya	1	90	2	5	0
Libo	0	67	0	0	0
Mecha	94	1	1	0	0
Mean (%)	**20.4**	**53**	**0.8**	**1.2**	**1.0**

SOURCE: Field Data

The data elicited from informants in this regard depict that the an average of 53% of the sample population uses rivers as a source of practicing irrigated agriculture, followed by over 20% who reported that they rely on dams for the same purpose. Use of other sources has been found negligible ranging from a minimum of 0.8% regarding use of wells to a maximum of 1.2% in terms of depending on streams. It was learnt that 94% of the respondents from Mecha and 90% of those in Dembiya affirmed that dams and rivers are the major means of practicing irrigated agriculture respectively. It could be stated that the existence of the government-led large-scale Koga Dam irrigation scheme has contributed to widespread use of dams in Mecha.

The aforementioned queries on specific types of sources for undertaking irrigation were followed by eliciting information on average irrigated land, amount of production in quintals per hectare and amount of cash income obtained from irrigated agricultural production crops produced through irrigation in 2004 EC in the sample *woredas* selected for the study (Table 3.29).

Table 3.29: Average irrigated land (ha), production/ha (quintals, and amount of income obtained in 2004 EC by sample *woreda*

Woreda	**Irrigated land (ha)**	**Yield/ha (quintal)**	**Income obtained from sale of products (Birr)**
Fogera	0.41	17.26	7478.22
Gondar Zuria	0.33	6.61	4365.00
Dembiya	0.43	7.38	3882.23
Libo	0.84	32.00	8299.02
Mecha	57.39	19.75	4999.30
Total Average	**11.85 (ha)**	**16.6 (quintals)**	**5804.75 (Birr)**

SOURCE: Field Data

The figures in Table 3.29 indicate that a total average of 11.85 hectares of agricultural land was irrigated in the sample *woredas* in 2004 EC. During the same production year, it was reported that 57.39 ha of land was irrigated in Mecha whereas in the remaining four the average size of irrigated land is highly negligible ranging from a minimum of 0.33 ha in Gondar Zuria to a maximum of 0.83 in Libo. One possible explanation for such a significant variation between Mecha and the other locations could be explained by the existence of the government-led Koga large- scale irrigation scheme located in the former. As regards volume of production, an average of 16.6 quintals/ha was produced. Among the sample *woredas*, Libo registered a maximum production of 32 quintals/ha. In the other locations, this ranged from a minimum of 6.6 quintals in Gondar Zuria to 19.75 quintals in Mecha.

With regard to the query whether farmers are aware of the ongoing government-sponsored irrigation schemes in and around the locations covered in the study, 87% of those questioned responded in the affirmative in the percentage range of a minimum of 62% in Gondar Zuria and 100% in Dembiya. The fact that 10% of the respondents from Mecha where the Koga large-scale irrigation scheme is found claimed ignorance of the subject is, however, surprising (Table 3.30).

Table 3.30: Percentage of respondents who are aware of ongoing irrigation schemes by *woreda*

Woreda	**%**
Fogera	94
Gondar Zuria	62
Dembiya	100
Libo	97
Mecha	90
Mean (%)	**87**

SOURCE: Field Data

One issue that was raised to informants was whether they expect benefits and other forms of positive outcomes resulting from the ongoing irrigation schemes in the locations studied. The percentage of informants who responded to this query in the affirmative is presented in Table 3.31.

Table 3.31: Percentage of respondents expecting positive outcomes from the irrigation schemes by *woreda*

Woreda	**%**
Fogera	2
Gondar Zuria	45
Dembiya	47
Libo	48
Mecha	0
Mean (%)	**28.4**

SOURCE: Field Data

It could be observed from the figures in Table 3.31 that an average of only 28.4% of the sample population in all the *woredas* expects to benefit from the schemes. This could be due to various reasons like loss of farmland to make way for the projects, inadequate compensation (if any), and similar other disaffections. When disaggregating the elicited response at the level of individual sample *woredas*, the percentage of affirmative responses obtained from respondents range between 2% in Fogera and 48% in Libo whereas no respondent from Mecha is reported as expecting positive outcomes from the ventures. Key informants in Mecha *woreda* mentioned the reluctance of farmers to exchange their land to irrigated land owing to profits earned from non-irrigated use of the land such as planting eucalyptus trees. Extension workers had to convince farmers to engage in irrigated schemes. In general, however, nearly 28% of the respondents indicated that they expect better income from the upcoming irrigation schemes---a clear indication of a positive attitude and receptivity to the scheme.

3.2 Livestock Production and Services

Data pertaining to the issue of livestock production and services were elicited from respondents in the *woredas* selected for the study focusing on ownership of livestock by type and breed, the state of livestock disease by type, access to and source of veterinary services, and the challenges militating against livestock production.

Information regarding ownership of livestock in the *woredas* is provided in Table 3.32. In terms of ownership, Libo and Mecha are in the lead where respondents from each reported ownership of a total of 542 animals including poultry and bee followed by Gondar Zuria, Dembiya and Fogera. The number of improved animals, however, are very small in all *woredas*.

Informants from the five sample *woredas* provided information on animal diseases that frequently affect their livestock. The frequency of responses obtained with regard to this is indicated in Table 3.33. Accordingly, animal diseases that frequently affect the health of livestock are *gendi* and *aba gorba*, among others, in order of severity with variations from *woreda* to *woreda*. In the case of the former (*gendi*), 67% of the respondents from Fogera, followed by those from Libo (38%), Dembiya (37%), and Gondar Zuria (19%) reported that their livestock are affected by the ailment whereas no one from Mecha mentioned being affected by this. Regarding the latter (*aba gorba*), 52% of the respondents from Fogera, followed by 13% in Dembiya, 12% in Gondar Zuria and 9% in Libo complained that their animals are affected by this disease. Again, no one from Mecha complained about the problem of animal health resulting from *aba gorba*.

Table 3.32: Livestock ownership by type, breed and study *woreda*

Type	**Fogera**		**Gondar Zuria**		**Dembiya**		**Libo**		**Mecha**		
	Local	**Impro -ved**	**Local**	**Impro -ved**	**Local**	**Impro -ved**	**Local**	**Impro -ved**	**Local**	**Impro ved**	**Total**
Cow	71	1	100	1	88	4	94	3	77	3	**442**
Oxen	66	0	100	1	90	1	89	0	89	1	**437**
Heifer	49	2	57	3	63	3	53	3	53	3	**289**
Bulls	39	0	34	0	29	2	53	2	35	2	**196**
Calves	56	0	51	0	17	0	66	2	60	9	**261**
Sheep	9	0	41	1	27	1	10	0	52	1	**142**
Goat	0	0	0	0	0	0	0	0	6	0	**6**
Horse	2	1	0	0	0	0	0	0	1	1	**5**
Donkey	48	1	44	0	43	0	57	0	18	0	**211**
Mules	1	0	0	0	3	0	1	0	22	0	**27**
Camels	1	1	0	0	2	0	1	0	0	0	**5**
poultry	83	8	78	4	84	1	83	8	89	4	**442**
Beehive	15	2	13	1	24	4	17	0	16	0	**92**
Total	**440**	**16**	**518**	**11**	**470**	**16**	**524**	**18**	**518**	**24**	**2555**

SOURCE: Field Data

Table 3.33: Percentage of respondents whose livestock have suffered from diseases by type of ailment and *woreda*

Type of disease	**Fogera**	**Gondar Zuria**	**Dembiya**	**Libo**	**Mecha**
Tryponomasis	0	0	0	0	0
Gendi	67	19	37	38	0
foot/mouth wound	4	4	9	12	0
Tuberculosis	1	1	2	1	1
Plouropen	0	0	0	0	1
Fasciolsis	2	0	2	0	0
Ticks	27	10	0	0	0
bird disease	0	0	0	0	0
i. parasite	0	3	0	3	7
e.parasite	0	1	0	0	0

sheep pox	0	0	1	0	3
external dependent	0	0	0	1	0
aba gorba	52	12	13	9	0
Gifaw	10	2	0	0	0
mitch/mariya	6	5	7	3	0
Other	2	10	0	0	0

SOURCE: Field Data

In this connection, an attempt was made to find out whether their animals affected by various health hazards received veterinary treatment. As indicated in Table 3.34, an average of over 61% of the respondents in all the locations confirmed that their ailing animals received treatment. Of these, 75% were from Mecha, followed by those in Gondar Zuria (66%), Fogera (65%), Libo (51%), and Dembiya (49%).

Table 3.34: Percentage of respondents whose animals got veterinary treatment by *woreda*

Woreda	%
Fogera	65
Gondar Zuria	66
Dembiya	49
Libo	51
Mecha	75
Mean	**61.2**

SOURCE: Field Data

Table 3.35 contains the percentage of respondents whose animals were treated through services provided by different providers of which government health extension systems are more frequently used by 65% of informants from Gondar Zuria. This is followed by 61%, 48 %, and 37% by those from Mecha, Fogera and Dembiya, and Libo respectively. Private veterinary clinics were reported as second source of service provision used by 15% of the informants in Fogera, and 14%, 12%, and 2% in Libo and Dembiya respectively whereas no one from Gondar Zuria mentioned using services of private providers.

Table 3.35: Percentage of respondents whose animals received veterinary treatment by sources of services and study *woreda*

Source of service	Fogera	Gondar Zuria	Dembiya	Libo	Mecha
Private vet. clinics	15	0	2	14	12
Government health extension	48	65	48	37	61
Farmers' cooperative	0	1	0	0	2
Other	5	0	0	0	1

SOURCE: Field Data

Informants approached in the study were asked to state the major constraints affecting their livestock production by ranking them in order of severity. Lack of grazing land as a major constraint was mentioned and ranked by respondents in the *woredas as indicated below* (Table 3.36).

Table 3.36: Percentage of respondents who faced major constraints relating to livestock production due to lack of grazing land by rank order and study *woreda*

	Lack of grazing land		
Woreda	**1st rank (%)**	**2nd rank (%)**	**3rd rank (%)**
Fogera	58	21	0
Gondar Zuria	71	25	1
Dembiya	93	1	0
Libo	52	39	3
Mecha	78	15	1
Mean (%)	**70.4**	**20.2**	**1**

SOURCE: Field Data

As shown in Table 3.36 , an average of 70.4% in the study *woredas* ranked lack of grazing land as first in order of severity. Of these an overwhelming majority of 93% were from Dembiya followed by those in Mecha (78%), Gondar Zuria (71%), Fogera (58%), and Libo (52%).

The figures in Table 3.37 depict the impact of lack of animal feed as a major constraint ranked by respondents in order of severity. An average of nearly 60% of the informants ranked lack of animal feed as the second major constraint to livestock production. Of these 71% were from Mecha and Gondar Zuria followed by those in Dembiya (60%), Libo (54%), and Fogera (42%).

Table 3.37: Percentage of respondents who faced major constraints relating to livestock production due to lack of animal feed by rank order and study *woreda*

	Lack of animal feed		
Woreda	**1st rank (%)**	**2nd rank (%)**	**3rd rank (%)**
Fogera	18	42	1
Gondar Zuria	21	71	2
Dembiya	25	60	3
Libo	41	54	2
Mecha	12	71	6
Mean (%)	**23.4**	**59.6**	**2.8**

SOURCE: Field Data

Informants stated that lack of veterinary service has severely constrained livestock production. The responses obtained in this regard are provided in Table 3.37 in which it is indicated that the impact of this problem is insignificant. Accordingly, an average of only 3% and less than 5% ranked this problem as 1st and 2nd respectively while an average of less that 13% ranked the problem as 3rd. Among those in the last category, 19% were those in Fogera and Mecha, 15% in Gondar Zuria, 10% in Libo, and only 1% in Dembiya.

Table 3.37: Percentage of respondents who faced major constraints relating to livestock production due to lack of vet services by rank order and study *woreda*

	Lack of veterinary service		
Woreda	**1st rank (%)**	**2nd rank (%)**	**3rd rank (%)**
Fogera	5	8	19
Gondar Zuria	3	4	15
Dembiya	2	3	1
Libo	3	1	10
Mecha	2	5	19
Mean (%)	**3**	**4.76**	**12.8**

SOURCE: Field Data

The issue of lack of quality breed and productive animals as having adversely affected livestock production was not stated by informants as a major constraint. The average percentage of responses putting the problem in the 1st and 2nd ranking order is 0.6% and 3.4% respectively (Table 3.38). The average percentage of those who ranked the problem as 3rd is less than 11% of which 31% are in Mecha.

Table 3.38: Percentage of respondents who faced major constraints relating to livestock production due to lack of quality breed by rank order and study *woreda*

	Lack of quality breed animals		
Woreda	**1st rank (%)**	**2nd rank (%)**	**3rd rank (%)**
Fogera	1	1	4
Gondar Zuria	1	1	2
Dembiya	0	4	7
Libo	0	0	8
Mecha	1	9	31
Mean (%)	**0.6**	**3.4**	**10.8**

SOURCE: Field Data

The average percentage of respondents who ranked the problem of lack of water as 1st and 2nd in terms of severity is 1.6% and 6.4% respectively whereas an average of less than 25% of respondents in the five *woredas* ranked the problem as 3rd. Among the latter, the highest figure of 62% is recorded in Dembiya followed by Libo (22%), Gondar Zuria (20%), Fogera 15%, and Mecha 5% (Table 3.39).

Table 3.39: Percentage of respondents who faced major constraints relating to livestock production due to lack of water by rank order and *woreda*

	Lack of water		
Woreda	**1st rank (%)**	**2nd rank (%)**	**3rd rank Mean (%)**
Fogera	5	10	15
Gondar Zuria	0	1	20
Dembiya	3	18	62
Libo	0	1	22
Mecha	0	2	5
Mean (%)	**1.6**	**6.4**	**24.8**

SOURCE: Field Data

As shown in Table 3.40, the problem of unfavorable topography in the form of steep landscape adversely affecting livestock production is highly negligible ranging from a minimum average of 0% as 1st to a maximum of less than 1% as 3rd in terms of severity.

Table 3.40: Percentage of respondents who faced major constraints relating to livestock production due to steep landscape by rank order and study *woreda*

	Steep Landscape		
Woreda	**1st rank (%)**	**2nd rank (%)**	**3rd rank (%)**
Fogera	0	0	0
Gondar Zuria	0	0	0
Dembiya	0	4	4
Libo	0	0	0
Mecha	0	0	0
Mean (%)	**0**	**0.8**	**0.8**

SOURCE: Field Data

The same is also true of menace by wild animals posing as a major constraint to livestock production (Table 3.41).

Table 3.41: Percentage of respondents who faced major constraints relating to livestock production due to menace by wild animals by rank order and study *woreda*

	Menace by wild animals		
Woreda	**1st rank**	**2nd rank**	**3rd rank**
Fogera	6	0	1
Gondar Zuria	0	0	0
Dembiya	1	0	1
Libo	0	0	0
Mecha	0	0	0
Mean (%)	**1.4**	**0**	**0.4**

SOURCE: Field Data

IV. ASSETS

The livelihood approach recognizes the importance of assets as the core of the household strategies to survive, meet their future needs or reduce their exposure to risks. Asset portfolios determine the levels of resilience and responsiveness to risks, shocks and events of households. In this study we examined two types of assets: Physical and Financial. Some details are provided below.

4.1 Physical Assets

Physical assets are understood here to mean both productive and household assets. The former, among others, includes tools and equipment households may use to generate income, livestock they possess and houses they own. Household assets refer to the various durable and non-durable items but in particular to valuables. Valuables such as jeweleries and other saleable items are hedges or insurance against risk.

4.1.1 *Productive Assets*

Table 4.1 shows almost all households possess house and livestock. The possession of house for rural households is not surprising since everybody can construct own houses on the plot he or she is given. In rural areas, the use of houses as productive assets however is very limited since people do not primarily engage in business activities. Livestock possession is also reported by an overwhelming majority where 97% reported to own livestock. Livestock asset can be used as a source of income since the sale of livestock products and livestock animals earn income to farmers (see below).

Households in the study *woredas* do not possess equipments and tools though they are important source of income and can help farmers to engage in non-farm activities. If households possess equipment, such as sewing machines and handicraft, they can easily manufacture products for sale or consumption.

Table 4.1: Percentage of Households Possessing Productive Assets in Different *woredas*

Woreda	House	Livestock	Car	Sewing machine	Handicraft loom
Dembia	99	97	1.0	0	0
Fogera	98	92	1.0	0	0
Gondar Zuria	100	98	0.0	0	0
Libokemekem	100	100	0.0	0	0
Mecha	95	97	5.0	2	0
Total	98.4	96.7	1.4	0.4	0

SOURCE: Field Data

4.1.2 *Household assets*

Possession of household asset indicates not only the standard of living enjoyed by the people but also the possibilities of using them as insurance or hedge against shocks. Table 4.2 shows that among the different electronic assets, radios and telephones are the ones owned by relatively higher proportion of people. On average about one-fifth of the sample own radios and a little less than one-third (30%) own telephones. The possession of these items is higher in Mecha and Libokemkem *woredas*. For example telephone is owned by nearly half or 48% in Libokemekem and by 41 % in Mecha. Similarly, 27% of households own radio in Libokemekem and 34% own the same in Mecha *woreda.* Both radios and telephones are significant means of communication and important sources of information. The fact that nearly one third possess telephone indicates the infiltration of mobile phones in rural Ethiopia which is increasingly being used for its economic value and for exchange of information on prices, This helps farmers attain a higher income.

Table 4.2: Percentage of Households Reporting Possession of household assets.

	Dembia	Fogera	Gondar Zuria	Libokemkem	Mecha	Total
TV	0	0	0	0	1	0.2
Radio	10.0	23.0	17.0	27.0	34.0	22.2
Tape recorder	5.0	3.0	3.0	7.0	11.0	5.8
Telephone	17.0	33.0	11.0	48.0	41.0	30.0
Refrigerators	2.0	3.0	0.0	1.0	0.0	1.2
Jewelry	40.0	62.0	61.0	95.0	89.0	69.4
Beds wooden/iron	96.0	84.0	95.0	96.0	90.0	92.2
Chairs	23.0	14.0	24.0	12.0	14.0	17.4
Table	1.0	1.0	0.0	9.0	2.0	2.6
Sofa	0.0	0.0	0.0	1.0	1.0	0.4
Electric Mitad	1.0	2.0	0.0	0.0	0.0	0.6
Cooking gas	0.0	1.0	0.0	2.0	0.0	0.6

SOURCE: Field Data

In terms of house items, most households (92%) seem to own beds which could be both wooden and iron. Other items such as chairs (17%) and Table s (3%) seem to be owned by less number of people. The most durable items that can be used by households any time as hedge against risk is jewelery. Surprisingly a very significant proportion of households (69%) possess jewelery. In *Woredas,* such as Libokemkem (95%) and Mecha (89%), the overwhelming majority possess jewelry.

The average prices households reported for the jewelry they possess is 709 birr while the highest is reported in Mecha *woreda* with 1112 birr (Table 4.3). Among the different items of household items, livestock seems to have a high value followed by house. The latter, however, can hardly be used as sources of income for rural people.

Table 4.3: Average prices of items owned by households

Woreda	Jewelry	House	Livestock	Telephone	radio	Beds
Dembia	343.5	8708.7	10567.5	427.6	201.0	294.1
Fogera	719.52	17433.5	23450.3	477.2	372.6	355.9
Gondar Zuria	475.08	17360.2	21871.1	488.2	157.3	248.4
Libokemkem	1111.96	23555.4	27151.8	495.8	212.8	754.6
Mecha	595.76	23578.1	15097.8	431.2	219.1	801.1
Total	708.90	18074.5	19544.1	466.3	238.3	491.5

SOURCE: Field Data

4.2 Financial Assets

Financial assets refer to the financial resources such as income, transfers, savings as well as credit. Income is the most important financial asset but income data, however, are very difficult to obtain as people are not willing to disclose their earnings. The following looks at savings and credit situation of households.

4.2.1 *Savings*

The study finds that only 23% of the rural households or 117 households save from their income. There is, however, some variation between *woredas* with Libokemkem being the one with the highest proportion of households with saving (45%) and Gondar Zuria being with the least proportion of households with savings (11%).

The average amount of saving reported by farmers is birr 3750.48 birr. There is, however, a considerable variation in the amount of savings among *woredas*. For example the average saving amount in Libokemkem (6244.66 birr) is ten times greater than the average saving amount of Dembia (653.64 birr). Since saving is generally a function of income, it can be surmised that the income levels of Libokemkem is much higher than other *woredas*.

Though banks (10.6%) seem to be the preferred places of savings, saving/credit union (6%) and home (5.2%) also serve as saving places for those who reported savings. In Libokemkem, where there is a high number of households with savings, banks (20%) and home (19%) are the two most preferred places. It is expected that savings in banks and in credit unions generate interests while others do not. In fact 74 respondents (64%) households out of the 117 households who reported savings indicated that they get interest from their saving which could be considered as additional income. The average income that accrued from interest in the last 12 months amounted to 186.87 birr with savers in Libokemkem receiving the highest amount (456.4 birr).

Households in rural areas do not practice equib. It is only three individuals who reported that they practice equib. These individuals must be closely living to the town where in general equib is highly practiced. For instance, in a livelihood study of urban households, Tegegne (OSSREA, 2011) found out that equib is practiced by 37 % of the urban poor households.

Table 4.4: Percentage of households with savings, place of savings and average amount of saving.

	Dembia	Fogera	Gondar Zuria	Libokeme kem	Mecha	Total
Proportion of Households with savings	12.0	22.0	11.0	45.0	27.0	23.4
Place of savings						
Bank	3.0	5.0	7.0	20.0	18.0	10.6
Saving/credit union	6.0	16.0	3.0	2.0	3.0	6.0
Home	2.0	1.0	1.0	19.0	3.0	5.2
Relatives and friends			0.0	2.0	0.0	0.4
Mean amount of savings	653.64	1117.82	1560.91	6244.66	4172.13	3750.48
Mean amount of interest received in the last 12 months	34.00	56.11	46.50	456.41	94.80	186.87

SOURCE: own survey

The majority of savers in different *woredas* (46%) reported that the major purpose is for household expenses. This is also true of all savers in all *woredas* except Fogera *woreda*. In Fogera *woreda*, the major purpose of saving is for investment in business (52.4%). In all other *woredas,* 16% of the savers reported that the objective of saving is for investing in business. It can, therefore, be seen that non-productive use of saving is predominant more than productive use in the areas studied.

Table 4.5: Expressed purpose of saving by savers in different *woredas*

	Dembia	Fogera	Gondar Zuria	Libokemkem	Mecha	Total
Housheohld expense	45.5 (5)	14.3 (3)	50.0 (5)	54.8 (23)	60.0 (9)	45.5 (45)
Medical expense	9.1 (1)	9.5 (2)	10.0 (1)	16.7 (7)	6.7 (1)	12.1 (12)
Children school	9.1 (1)	4.8 (1)	30.0 (3)	2.4 (1)	33.3 (5)	11.1 (11)
Buy land	27.3 (3)	0.0 (0)	0.0 (0)	2.4 (1)	0.0 (0)	4.0 (4)
Buy/build house	0.0 (0)	4.8 (1)	0.0 (0)	16.7 (7)	0.0 (0)	8.1 (8)
Invest in business	9.1 (1)	52.4 (11)	10.0 (1)	7.1 (3)	0.0 (0)	16.2 (16)
Others (specify)	0.0 (0)	14.3 (3)	0.0 (0)	0.0 (0)	0.0 (0)	3.0 (3)
N	11	21	10	42	15	99*

*Note that the number of respondents who specified the purpose of savings is 18 less than the 117 respondents who reported to have savings.

Numbers in parenthesis are number of reporting respondents

4.2.2 *Credit*

Borrowing or drawing credit is not a major part of rural households' life. It is only 36 individuals or 7.2 % of the total households who reported borrowing in the last three months. Further, 20 individuals or 57% of those who borrowed indicated that they borrowed from organizations while 15 individuals or 43% mentioned that their sources of credit are friends or persons they know. Among those who borrowed from organizations, 16 individuals (84%) borrowed from credit unions and the rest took from service cooperatives while among those who borrowed from people whom they know , 10 individuals (77%) borrowed from relatives. It thus appears that credit unions and relatives remain to be the most important sources of credit for rural households. The latter are informal sources and hence their reliability and adequacy in providing credit is questionable and the arrangements between the credit providers and credit receivers are not also standard.

The dominant mode of loan payment is by paying lump sum (75%) while paying in installments is practiced by 25% of the borrowers. Lump sum payment puts pressure on borrowers as they have to service the debt in one go. A significant proportion (86%) of borrowers also reported as having an outstanding debt. The pattern in modes of payment and presence of outstanding debt is similar across all *woredas*.

Table 4.6: Percentage of respondents who borrowed, mode of payment and outstanding debt

	Dembia	Fogera	Gondar Zuria	Libokemkem	Mecha	Total
HH who borrowed in the last 3 months	4.0	18.0	7.0	4.0	3.0	7.2
	(4)	(18)	(7)	(4)	(3)	(36)
Source of loan*						
Organizations	75.0	70.6	14.3	75.0	33.3	57.1
	(3)	(12)	(1)	(3)	(1)	(20)
Persons	25.0	29.4	85.7	256.0	66.6	42.9
	(1)	(5)	(6)	(1)	(2)	(15)
Mode of loan payment						
Lump sum	100.0	66.7	71.4	75.0	100.0	75.0
	(4)	(12)	(5)	(3)	(3)	(27)
Installment	0.0	33.3	28.6	25.0	0.0	25.0
		(6)	(2)	(1)		(9)
Outstanding debt						
Yes	75.0	94.4	57.1	100.0	100.0	85.7
	(3)	(17)	(4)	(4)	(2)*	(30)
No	25.0	5.6	42.9	0.0	0.0	14.3
	(1)	(1)	(3)			(5)

*One person did not give answer to this question

Despite the fact that credit plays a role in only a few households, the amount of money borrowed however signifies that for those who borrowed on credit for the business is quite significant. The average amount of money borrowed in the past three months is 2333.4 birr.

Table 4.7 Mean amount of borrowing in the last past months

Woreda	Mean amount borrowed in the last three months	N
Dembia	1825.0	4
Fogera	3305.9	17
Gondar Zuria	478.57	7
Libokemkem	2754.5	4
Mecha	1266.67	3
Total	2333.40	35*

*Note that one individual did not respond to the amount of money borrowed

Farmers in Libokemkem have taken the highest amount of loan (2754 birr) while those in Gondar Zuria have limited borrowing (479 birr). Farmers in Libokemkem have taken the highest amount of loan (2754 birr) while those in Gondar Zuria have limited borrowing (479 birr).Loans are mainly taken for buying cattle (30.6%), purchase food (19.4%) and other reasons (19.4%).

Table 4.8: Percentage of borrowers by purpose of loan

Purpose of loan	Frequency	Percentage
Purchase food	7	19.4
Medical expense	1	2.8
Children school	1	2.8
Buy cloth	3	8.3
Buy land	1	2.8
Buy/build house	3	8.3
Buy cattle	11	30.6
Invest in business	1	2.8
Other	7	19.4

SOURCE: Field Data

V. HOUSING AND HEALTH

5.1 Housing Characteristics

Housing is an important indicator of the quality of life. It has important connection with household income/wealth and health status of its members. The quality of indoor environment is closely related with the incidence and severity of different diseases. In- door sanitary conditions also affect food contamination contributing to high incidence of food borne diseases. The following describes the structure of housing units, crowding of housing units and indoor sanitation.

5.1.1 Structure of housing units

The structure of a housing unit relates to a dimension of housing that mainly relates to a) the quality and type of building materials used for the wall, roof, floor and ceiling, b) the number of stories in the building and c) the number of attached housing units used by different households. These elements affect the extent to which the housing units protect its occupants from different factors that affect the health of household members.

In the areas studied, there are no attached housing units or buildings with multi stories. All houses are also made of mud floors and the walls are also made of wood and mud. In the light of this, the only indicator used in this study to denote the structure of housing units is the type of building material used for roofs. Table 5.1 shows that about 90% of the households own tin roofed houses and it is only 10 % who live in thatched houses. In rural Ethiopia, tin roofed houses are afforded by those with high levels of income. The fact that the overwhelming majority possess tin roofed house is an indication of improvement in the lives of rural people. The majority of the households in the areas studied can therefore afford tin-roofed houses. There is slight variation in the proportion of households with tin roofed houses among all *woredas*. The only exception is Fogera where 80 % as opposed to over 90% in other *woredas* reported tin roofed houses.

Table 5.1: Percentage distribution of respondents by type of roof

Woreda	Tin roofed		Thatch	
	No	%	No	%
Dembia	89	91.8	8	8.2
Fogera	78	79.6	20	20.4
Gondar Zuria	91	91.9	9	8.1
Libokemkem	87	89.7	10	10.3
Mecha	98	98.0	2	2.0
Total	443	90.2	48	9.8

SOURCE: Field Data

5.1.2 *Crowding of housing units*

The extent of crowding in the sample households is measured by the number of rooms per housing units and person-room ratio in each household. The majority or about half (50%) of the houses are two-room houses while about one-fourth (24.7%) have more than two rooms and the remaining one-fourth (24.9%) have only one room. Houses with more than two rooms are prevalent in Mecha (57.0%) while houses with one-room are prevalent in Dembia (58%).

Table 5.2: Housing Characteristics- number of rooms and persons per room

Woreda	One		Two		More than two		Persons per room	
	No	%	No	%	No	%	Mean	SD
Dembia	56	57.7	32	33.0	9	9.3	4.01	1.82
Fogera	25	25.0	62	62.0	13	13.0	3.04	1.35
Gondar Zuria	19	19.2	57	57.6	23	23.2	2.97	1.35
Libokemkem	14	14.4	63	64.9	20	20.6	2.62	0.94
Mecha	9	9.0	34	34.0	57	57.0	2.32	0.71
Total	123	24.9	248	50.3	122	24.7	2.99	1.40

SOURCE: Field Data

The persons per room shows the extent to which the area is characterized by a large person-room ratio (2.99). Dembia (4.01) and Fogera (3.04) have much higher person-room ratio indicating a significant level of crowding.

5.1.3 *Indoor Sanitation*

With respect to indoor sanitary conditions, the survey instrument included questions regarding the place used to cook food or whether there is a separate kitchen and questions regarding the place where livestock are kept in the night.

In terms of kitchen, the population is split into two in that nearly half (51.5%) reported to have separate kitchen while the remaining nearly half (48.5%) of the sample reported to have no kitchen. Households in Mecha *woreda* where most of them have more than two rooms have more number of households with kitchen (68%) as opposed to households in Gondar Zuria (59.6%) and Dembia (58.8%) where the majority of households have no kitchen. In Dembia the majority of households have only one-room houses though this is not true of Gondar Zuria. Households with no separate kitchen will be forced to use in-door or out-door for cooking purposes. In the case of the former, cooking food in-door will have significant implications on health.

Table 5.3: Proportion of households indicating presence of separate kitchens

	Houses with separate kitchens		Houses with no separate kitchens	
	No	%	No	%
Dembia	39	40.6	57	59.4
Fogera	59	59.0	41	41.0
Gondar Zuria	41	41.4	58	58.6
Libokekem	47	48.0	51	52.0
Mecha	68	68.0	32	32.0
Tota	254	51.5	239	48.5

SOURCE: Field Data

Table 5.4 shows that small animals such as sheep, goats and hens, stay in the house at night. For example, 83% of the households mentioned that they keep their small animals at house at night. It is only 12% of the households who keep their small animals in barns. With regard to large animals, such as cows and equines, a significant proportion of the households (41%) mentioned that they keep them in barns while a similar proportion of households (46%) keep them in houses.

The above findings indicate that for a significant proportion of households animals stay in the house at night. This will have health impacts on human beings since the chances for the house to be unhygienic are high.

Table 5.4 : Percentage of respondents indicating the places where animals stay at night

	Cows and equines				Sheep, goats and hens			
	House	Kitchen	Barns	Open field	House	Kitchen	Barns	Open field
Dembia	26.6	2.1	62.8	7.4	88.6	0.0	6.8	4.5
Fogera	75.8	1.1	13.2	9.9	89.2	1.1	9.7	0.0
Gondar zuria	27.1	6.2	52.1	14.6	85.9	1.1	10.9	2.2
Libokekem	62.1	15.8	13.7	7.4	82.6	14.0	2.3	0.0
Mecha	38.1	0.0	61.9	0.0	67.3	6.1	26.5	0.0
Total	45.7	5.1	41.0	7.8	82.5	4.4	11.6	1.3

SOURCE: Field Data

The sleeping arrangement of the family members could be used as indicator of the standard of living. Those families who cannot afford to have separate rooms use the same room for all members of the family as sleeping places. In some instances all family members can use the same bed at night. Table 5.5 shows that 50% of all households use the same room as sleeping place while 35% use different bed rooms. The majority thus cannot afford to have separate bed rooms for children and spouses. As indicated above, the average family size is 5 and the fact that all members sleep in the same room could be considered as instances of overcrowding.

Woreda variation is significant in that a significant proportion of households in Mecha (70%) and Gondar zuria (43%) have separate rooms for children and spouses. On the other hand in Libokemekem (57%) and Dembia (100%) a significant proportion of households reported the use of the same room for children and spouses.

Table 5.5: Percentage distribution of respondents indicating the sleeping arrangement of spouses and children in the house

	Spouses and children sleep in the same room sharing the same bed	Spouses and children sleep in the same room but use different beds	Spouses and other members of the family sleep in different rooms
Dembia	0.0	100.0	0.0
Fogera	25.3	34.3	37.4
Gondar Zuria	10.5	45.3	43.2
Libokemekem	20.0	57.0	21.0
Mecha	13.0	16.0	70.0
Total	13.9	50.2	34.5

SOURCE: Field Data

5.2 Family health status

Health status of a household is an important indicator and determinant of the welfare of its members. Health status also determines the capacity of households to earn their livelihood and build their human capital.

5.2.1 *Household perception of health status and presence of recurrent diseases*

Household perception of health status is a subjective measure of illness. It may have some variance with the objective measure of illness. Subjective measures however could be used as indicators of household behavior regarding their illness. Table 5.6 shows that 79.5 % of the households perceive that their health status is very good or good. It is only 10 % who felt that they have poor health conditions. It is assumed that the perception depends on the health feeling individuals might have. Accordingly, those who perceive good health may not seek treatment. As indicated above, however, perception may not tally with medical evidences about the health of individuals.

Despite the fact that over three quarter of household feel that they have good health, nearly two-third of the households reported that they have been attacked by recurrently occurring diseases. In some *woredas,* such as in Dembia, the presence of diseases frequently attacking members is reported by nearly 80% of the households. Malaria being reported by 65% seems to be the most prevalent recurrently attacking disease in the area. The same disease is reported by 77% in Dembia. The reason for this is that as the area is found in the shores of Lake Tana, most of the places are low lying and suffer from flooding problem particularly in places like Fogera. Cough (12.3%) and TB (7.9%) are other diseases reported by households as recurrently occurring diseases.

Table 5.6: Perception of health status, presence and types of recurrent diseases

	Dembia	Fogera	Gondar Zuria	Libokemekem	Mecha	Total
Perception about family health						
Excellent	3.1	20.0	6.2	0.0	23.2	10.7
Very good	32.3	30.0	39.2	48.9	41.4	38.3
Good	51.0	29.0	41.2	51.1	34.3	41.2
poor	13.5	21.0	13.4	0.0	1.0	9.9
Presence of diseases recurrently attacking family members						
Yes	78.9	70.0	68.0	62.8	43.3	64.4
No	20.0	29.0	30.9	37.2	55.7	34.7
Type of diseases recurrently attacking family members						
Cough	6.0	17.2	18.1	10.8	8.8	12.3
Tuberclosis (TB)	10.8	3.1	4.2	13.8	5.9	7.9
Malaria	77.1	54.7	61.1	64.6	61.8	64.8
Typhus	2.4	0.0	4.2	1.5	11.8	3.1
Other	3.6	25.0	12.5	9.2	11.8	11.9

SOURCE: Field Data

5.2.2 *Maternal death*

Maternal death in the last 5 years was reported by 6% of the household (Table 5.7). This is an indication that maternal death is not a common phenomenon in the study sites. Differences among *woredas* are not significant in this regard. For those who experienced maternal death, the major reason seems to be lack of proper maternal care at the time of delivery.

Table 5.7: Maternal death and possible causes for death*.

	Dembia	Fogera	Gondar Zuria	Liboke mkem	Mecha	Total
Presence of maternal death in the last 5 years	2.1	8.0	4.2	8.2	6.1	5.8
Causes of death						
Lack of proper maternal care at the time of delivery	0.0	4.0	4.0	5.0	1.0	3.0
Attempted abortion	0.0	0.0	0.0	0.0	1.0	0.2
Other	0.0	0.0	0.0	0.0	3.0	0.6

*Out of those who indicated presence of maternal death, some did not mention the causes of death.

5.2.3 *Utilization of health care services*

One of the problems of the health sector in rural Ethiopia is the low level of utilization of preventive as well as curative health services. Table 5.8 depicts that in case of family sickness, the majority of households (58%) sought treatment in health posts, clinics and health stations. In some *woredas*, such as Dembia (76%) and Libokemekem (72%), the proportions are even much higher. This is a positive trend and needs to be encouraged. There are, however, a significant proportion of households (39%) who did not seek any treatment. There could be many possible reasons for this. Lack of awareness and lack of finance may be some of the possible reasons for such behavior. It is therefore important to identify the root causes in order to design remedial alternatives since health centers remain to be critical facilities that need to be visited in case of sickness.

Table 5.8: Percentage of households by type of treatment sought for family sickness

	Dembia	Fogera	Gondar Zuria	Libokemekem	Mecha	Total
No treatment	19.0	39.8	46.2	19.0	60.2	39.2
Went to traditional facilities	0.0	4.1	0.0	8.6	1.0	2.4
Went to clinics, health posts and health centers	75.9	56.1	53.8	72.4	38.8	57.5
Other	5.1	0.0	0.0	0.0	0.0	0.9
N	79	98	91	58	98	424

SOURCE: Field Data

Similarly the use of preventive services is critical to fight against diseases. Table 5.9 shows that nearly 74% of the households indicated that they have got their children vaccinated. The proportion is higher for Fogera (77%) and Gondar Zuria (75%). There are, however, a substantial proportion (27%) who did not get their children vaccinated.

Table 5.9 Proportion of households who got children vaccinated

Households who got their children vaccinated	Dembia	Fogera	Gondar Zuria	Libokemkem	Mecha	Total
Yes	67.0	77.3	75.0	63.3	86.9	73.5
No	33.0	22.7	25.0	36.7	13.1	26.5
N	97	97	96	98	84	472

SOURCE: Field Data

5.2.4 *Food consumption habits*

The food consumption habit of household members is an important determinant of health status. This is because the quantity and composition of diet determine the micro nutrient intake needed for a healthy functioning of the people concerned. Table 5.10 shows the frequency of consuming meat in the family. Most household (92%) reported that they do not eat meat at all while only 6% consume meat on holidays. There is no major difference among *woredas* in this regard. The fact that households never use meat indicates the extent of poor nourishment in the family's diet.

Table 5.10: Percentage distribution of respondents by frequency of meat consumption in the family

	Dembia	Fogera	Gondar zuria	Libokekem	Mecha	Total
More than once in a week	0.0	1.0	0.0	0.0	0.0	0.2
Once in two weeks	0.0	2.2	0.0	0.0	0.0	0.
Once in a month	1.0	0.0	3.0	3.2	0.0	1.4
On holidays	1.0	10.1	7.1	0.0	13.3	6.3
Never	98.0	86.9	89.9	96.8	86.7	91.6
N	98	99	99	95	98	489

SOURCE: Field Data

The quantity of food intake is approximated by using the number of meals per day for adults and children. Table 5.11 shows that the number of meals is higher for children than for adults. About 62 % of the total households reported that children have four meals per day as opposed to 76% of households who reported three meals for adults. The pattern across *woredas* is similar except Mecha *woreda* where a significant proportion of households (75%) reported that children have three meals per day.

Table 5.11: Proportion of households indicating number of meals per day

	Number of meals per day adults				Number of meals per day, children			
	One	two	three	four	one	Tow	three	four
Dembia	1.0	7.0	89.0	3.0	1.0	0.0	10.1	88.9
Fogera	0.0	10.1	84.8	5.1	2.2	2.2	25.6	70.0
Gondar zuria	0.0	23.2	76.8	0.0	0.0	4.4	37.8	57.8
Libokemkem	0.0	24.0	71.0	5.0	0.0	0.0	22.5	77.5
Mecha	0.0	42.0	58.0	0.0	0.0	7.1	74.7	18.2
Total	0.2	21.3	75.9	2.6	0.6	2.8	34.5	62.1

VI. INCOME AND EXPENDITURE

6.1 Sale and Purchase of Crops

The most important source of income for most farmers is selling farm products. Farmers also purchase items required for household consumption. This section reports farmers' practice of selling and purchasing of crops and their food status.

With regard to the sale of crops during the year in question, the percentage of respondents who sold crop, types of crops sold, income obtained thereof in each *woreda* is provided in Table 6.1.

Table 6.1: Percentage of respondents who sold crops in 2004 E.C. by type, average value (in birr), and *woreda*

Type	Fogera		Gondar Zuria		Dembiya		Libo		Mecha	
	%	Av. Value	%	Av. value	%	Av. value	%	Av. value	%	Av. value
Teff	15	2753	63	2917	96	4239	1	1000	42	2328
Barley	5	2780	3	766	67	3213	0	0	39	849
Maize	3	2636	6	621	61	2434	18	1075	69	2612
Millet	5	1200	4	1745	39	2375	30	3125	12	908
Wheat	5	5750	4	1526	11	2300	4	3050	74	2657
sorghum	2	7425	20	805	23	2051	2	5500	6	83
Finger millet	1	2960	0	0	15	1966	4	6150	2	2050
Oats	65	3909	11	1631	15	4433	45	5102	34	2726
fenugreek	2	3175	2	1700	4	1425	1	1600	0	0
pepper	35	3600	1	2000	19	1100	16	3441	9	1770
oilseeds	4	1100	4	1137	14	2845	51	1056	9	582

SOURCE: Field Data

The data in Table 6.1 indicates that informants from the five *woredas* studied sold various crops and earned incomes resulting thereof. In Fogera, the majority (65%) sold oats followed by sale of pepper and teff undertaken by 35% and teff 15% respectively. In Gondar Zuria, teff was sold by 63% of respondents followed by sale of sorghum and oats by 20% and 11% of the informants respectively. The overwhelming majority of 96% in Dembiya sold teff followed by barley and maize sold by 67% and 61% respectively. A majority of 51% in Libo sold oil seeds whereas the percentage of respondents who sold oats and millet was reported to be 45% and 30% respectively. A majority of households in Mecha (74%) sold wheat followed by 69% and 42% who sold maize and teff respectively.

The foregoing therefore indicates that a significant proportion of farmers are engaged in selling one or another type of crops. Teff and oats however seem to be the most important crops brought to market.

In terms of the income the average income earned is 805 and 7425 birr for those who sold sorghum in Gondar zuria and Fogera *woredas* respectively. It appears that those in Dembia have obtained higher income from selling crops since many farmers have reported crop sales.

By the same token, the figures in Table 6.2 illustrate that respondents in the locations studied purchased various crops in 2004 E.C.

Table 6.2 : Percentage of respondents who purchased crops in 2004 EC by type, value (in birr), and *woreda*

Type	**Fogera**		**Gondar Zuria**		**Dembiya**		**Libo**		**Mecha**	
	%	**Av. value**	**%**	**Av. value**	**%**	**Av. value**	**%**	**Av. value**	**%**	**Av. value**
Teff	23	1484	7	450	1	1200	41	1306	40	660
Barley	3	300	2	245	6	284	56	495	1	420
Maize	57	1067	2	1575	14	1165	66	972	6	1150
Millet	5	1250	0	0	1	1000	29	852	12	950
Wheat	4	287	0	0	1	132	5	450	0	0
Sorghum	23	1208	40	1782	5	1420	0	0	0	0
Finger millet	17	1139	0	0	2	650	13	883	1	300
Oats	0	0	3	333	0	0	1	600	1	300
fenugreek	0	0	1	198	0	0	0	0	0	0
Pepper	55	606	65	400	36	384	88	625	76	511
oilseeds	1	1800	2	387	2	46	4	962	0	0

SOURCE: Field Data

In 2004 E.C, it was reported that 57% of the informants in Fogera purchased maize followed by 55% and 23% each who bought pepper, teff and sorghum respectively. A majority of 65% in Gondar Zuria purchased pepper followed by 40% regarding sorghum. A maximum of 36% respondents in Dembiya purchased pepper followed by 14% who bought maize during the period in question. In Libo, 88% purchased pepper followed by 66% and 56% of those who bought maize and barley respectively whereas the percentage of respondents in this category in Mecha ranges from a minimum of 1% (barley, finger millet, and oats) and a maximum of 76% (pepper).

6.2 Sales and Purchase of Livestock and Livestock Products

With regard to the query whether respondents have sold livestock, including poultry and beehives, and the amount of revenue obtained thereof, the responses are indicated in Table 6.3.

Table 6.3: Sale of livestock in 2004 EC by type, number and value and *woreda*

Type	Fogera		Gondar Zuria		Dembiya		Libo		Mecha	
	No.	Value (birr)	No.	Value (birr)	No.	Value (birr)	No.	Value (Birr)	No.	Value (birr)
Cow	14	3285	16	2255	13	2133	17	2984	3	4066
Oxen	26	6081	27	3854	31	4994	34	5494	41	6817
heifer	2	2250	11	938	6	1183	9	1744	5	1730
Bulls	7	2285	12	2473	2	833	0	0	3	1700
calves	5	920	0	0	0	0	5	1575	2	780
Sheep	4	1800	24	1300	10	1760	5	960	40	1027
Goat	7	1103	4	2225	0	0	0	0	3	4600
Horse	0	0	0	0	0	0	0	0	0	0
Donkey	12	1233	5	1140	5	1200	10	1393	1	750
Mule	0	0	0	0	0	0	1	1750	4	5966
Camel	0	0	0	0	0	0	0	0	0	0
poultry	48	100	35	209	21	299	31	279	74	328
Beehive	1	1200	0	0	0	0	0	0	0	0
Total	**126**	**20257**	**134**	**14394**	**88**	**12402**	**46**	**16119**	**175**	**27704**

SOURCE: Field Data

With regard to the number of livestock including poultry and beehives sold in 2004 EC, the data in Table 6.3 indicate that a total of 175 respondents in Mecha sold livestock followed by Gondar Zuria, Fogera, Dembiya and Libo. In terms of revenues obtained from sale during the year in question, informants from Mecha received the highest revenue amounting to Birr 27704 followed by those from Fogera, Libo, Gondar Zuria, and Dembiya in descending order of income obtained from sale respectively. Concerning the question whether informants have purchased livestock including poultry and beehives in 2004 EC, the responses elicited are illustrated in Table 6.4. Accordingly, it was reported that informants from Libo took the lead with regard to the number of livestock purchased (11) followed by Fogera (8), Dembiya (7), Gondar Zuria (6), and Mecha (5). In terms of the amount of money expended for purchase, those from Fogera spent the highest by paying Birr 6876 followed by those from Gondar Zuria, Dembiya, Mecha, and Libo in descending order of money expended for purchase of livestock respectively.

Table 6.4: Purchase of livestock in 2004 EC by type, number, value and *woreda*

Type	**Fogera**		**Gondar Zuria**		**Dembiya**		**Libo**		**Mecha**	
	No.	**value (birr)**	**No.**	**value (birr)**	**No.**	**value (birr)**	**No.**	**value (birr)**	**No.**	**value (birr)**
Cow	5	4200	4	4375	5	2920	8	1075	2	4750
Oxen	0	0	0	0	0	0	0	0	0	0
Heifer	3	2666	2	2300	2	3237	3	3166	3	750
Bulls	0	0	0	0	0	0	0	0	0	0
Calves	0	0	0	0	0	0	0	0	0	0
Sheep	0	0	0	0	0	0	0	0	0	0
Goat	0	0	0	0	0	0	0	0	0	0
Horse	0	0	0	0	0	0	0	0	0	0
Donkey	0	0	0	0	0	0	0	0	0	0
Mules	0	0	0	0	0	0	0	0	0	0
Camels	0	0	0	0	0	0	0	0	0	0
Poultry	0	0	0	0	0	0	0	0	0	0
Beehives	0	0	0	0	0	0	0	0	0	0
Total	**8**	**6876**	**6**	**6675**	**7**	**6157**	**11**	**4241**	**5**	**5500**

SOURCE: Field Data

The issue of obtaining income from animal products was also one of the focal areas of this baseline survey. Data pertaining to this are illustrated in Table 6.5.

Table 6.5: Frequency of sold animal products by type, income earned in 2004 EC, and study *woreda*

Type	Fogera		Gondar Zuria		Dembiya		Libo		Mecha	
	Freq.	Income (birr)	Freq.	Income (birr	Freq.	Income (birr	Freq.	Income (birr)	Freq.	Income (birr
Milk	2	25	0	0	0	0	0	0	0	0
Eggs	65	180	100	91	73	11	53	53	43	52
Honey	8	93	99	49	62	33	51	43	28	20
Butter	24	535	100	229	75	346	61	97	23	193
Hides/ Skin	16	64	100	14	50	10	57	15	44	48
Other	0	0	0	0	0	0	0	0	0	0
Total	**115**	**897**	**399**	**383**	**260**	**400**	**222**	**208**	**138**	**313**

SOURCE: Field Data

As shown in the figures in Table 6.5, eggs, butter, honey and hides/skins were the most frequently sold animal products in the *woredas* covered by the study in 2004 EC from which the highest income amounting to Birr 897 was earned in Fogera followed by Dembiya, Gondar Zuria, Mecha and Libo in descending order of obtained revenue respectively.

6.3 Household Expenditure

The consumption patterns of households in two weeks time for which they have good collection indicates that the most important consumption items are coffee/tea (90.4%), cooking oil/fat (90.2%), detergent (83.4%), matches/candles (74%) and sugar/salt (63%) (Table 6.6). Meat, kerosene and grain/flour are purchased by less number of households while other items such as pasta, rice and tobacco are consumed by an insignificant proportion of households.

Table 6.6 Consumption in two weeks time

Item	Dembia	Fogera	Gondar Zuria	Libokemkem	Mecha	Total
Grains / Flour	0	3	16	24	86	25.8
Rice	0	0	0	1	0	0.2
Pasta	0	1	0	1	1	0.6
Sugar / salt	64	58	60	72	60	62.8
Tea / Coffee	94	94	93	91	80	90.4
Matches/candles	95	52	70	86	66	73.8
Cooking oil / fat	98	91	91	92	79	90.2
Beans	6	3	2	0	2	2.6
Vegetables, Onions / Potatoes	57	44	56	37	79	54.6
Meat / Milk	85	39	31	1	72	45.6
Tobacco / Snuff/ Mirra	3	6	0	2	3	2.8
Detergent (Soap/omo)	73	81	96	80	87	83.4
Kerosene	81	48	46	36	67	55.6

SOURCE: Field Data

Meat/milk is consumed by less than half of the households but commands the highest expenditure for those reporting meat/milk consumption. Similarly, grain/flour is purchased by a quarter of the households and the average expenditure is about 79 birr. Other items in order of average expenditure are tea/coffee (40 birr) and kerosene (36birr). More details are provided in Table 6.7.

Table 6.7: Average amount of expenditure for two weeks consumption

Item	Dembia	Fogera	Gondar Zurai	Libokemkem	Mecha	Total
Grains / Flour	-	423.3	80.81	143.72	47.78	79.20
Sugar / salt	8.06	20.64	12.00	17.8	17.38	15.14
Tea / Coffee	41.4	34.27	33.18	35.11	56.11	39.56
Matches/candles	1.35	2.44	1.96	1.98	3.46	2.13
Cooking oil / fat	25.96	44.23	24.35	52.04	34.13	36.07
Vegetables / Onions / Potatoes	13.75	14.67	11.33	27.86	10.15	14.27
Meat / Milk	107.35	158.56	96.77	25.00	173.43	135.17
Detergent (Soap/omo)	7.00	13.66	9.57	16.91	13.52	12.15
Kerosene	8.15	41.04	9.42	28.58	13.16	17.83

Table 6.8 shows where rural households expend or from where rural households source different expenditure items. Grains/flour (45%), matches/candles (50%), meat/milk (79%) and vegetables/onions and potatoes (50%) are sourced from rural areas. On the other hand, sugar/salt (67%), cooking oil (68%), detergents (70%) and keorsene (71%) are mainly sourced from *woreda* town.

Table 6.8: Percentage of respondents by location of expenditure items

Item	Rural	*woreda* town	Other towns	Bahirdar	Total
Grains / Flour	45.0	51.1	*3.8*	-	*100*
	(59)	(67)	*(5)*		*(131)*
Sugar /salt	17.3	67.3	*15.3*		*100*
	(52)	(202)	*(46)*		*(300)*
Tea / Coffee	44.9	37.0	*18.1*		*100*
	(188)	(155)	*(76)*		*(419)*
Matches/candles	50.2	35.6	*14.2*		*100*
	(166)	(118)	*(47)*		*(331)*
Cooking oil / fat	13.9	68.2	*17.7*	*0.2*	*100*
	(58)	(285)	*(74)*	*(1)*	*(418)*
Beans					
Vegetables	50.2	42.7	*6.7*	*0.4*	*100*
/ Onions / Potatoes	(127)	(108)	*(17)*	*(1)*	*(253)*
Meat / Milk	79.2	17.4	*3.4*		*100*
	(164)	(36)	*(7)*		*(207)*
Tobacco					
/ Snuff/ Mirra					
Detergent	16.2	69.6	*14.1*		*100*
(Soap/omo)	(62)	(266)	*(54)*		*(382)*
Kerosene	16.4	71.2	*12.4*		*100*
	(71)	(178)	*(31)*		*(252)*

SOURCE: Field Data

VII. RURAL URBAN LINKAGE, NON-FARM ACTIVITIES AND FOOD STATUS

7.1 Travel to towns

Farmers have increasingly become multi-spatial and multi-sectoral in deriving their livelihood. One of the manifestations of the multi-spatial nature of farmers is the linkages farmers exhibit with towns. Such linkage involves mobility by rural people to the nearest urban centers for different purposes. The frequency of travel and the purpose of travel are indicative of the linkage farmers have with the urban centers.

Table 7.1 and FIG 2 show the frequency of travel to towns by rural households. Accordingly, the proportion of husbands travelling to towns 1-2 times a week is 59% and that of wives is 42.5%. In comparison with husbands, wives seem to have less frequency of travel to towns. For example 36% of wives visit towns once in two weeks while the percentage of husbands visiting towns once in two weeks is 28%. Similarly 4% of wives visit once in two months while husbands in this category are only 1%

Table 7.1 Frequency of travel to towns by husband and wife

		Dembia	Fogera	Gondar Zuria	Libokemkem	Mecha	Total
Every day	husband	0.0	1.1	0.0	0.0	1.1	0.4
	wife	0.0	1.0	1.0	0.0	1.0	0.6
1-2 times a week	husband	61.9	50.5	74.7	66.0	41.1	59.2
	wife	47.3	39.4	40.8	26.0	58.6	42.5
Once in two weeks	husband	36.1	30.5	19.2	22.3	33.3	28.2
	wife	49.5	28.3	40.8	27.1	33.3	35.7
Once in a month	husband	1.0	10.5	5.1	2.1	14.4	6.5
	wife	3.2	11.1	14.3	17.7	3.0	9.9
Once in two months	husband	0.0	3.2	0.0	0.0	3.3	1.3
	wife	0.0	4.0	2.0	13.5	1.0	4.1
Never	husband	1.0	1.1	0.0	1.1	3.3	1.3
	wife	0.0	4.0	0.0	3.1	2.0	1.9
As need arises	husband	0.0	3.2	0.0	8.5	3.3	3.2
	wife	0.0	12.1	1.0	12.5	1.0	5.4
N	husband	97	95	99	94	90	475
	wife	99	99	98	96	99	485

SOURCE: Field Data

The towns visited by most households are *woreda* capitals (see Table 7.2). Koladiba, Woreta, Teda, Merawi are all *woreda* towns and are visited by many households. In addition to these *woreda* towns, however, there are other places which are also visited by farmers. These include Robit for hosueholds in Dembia, Yefiga, and Alember for households in Woreta and Arbete for households in Mecha. Households from Fogera and Libokemekem, which are neighboring *Woredas,* seem to be attracted to some common towns such as Woreta and Yifiga. Sample respondents in Libokemkem did not report a visit to Addis Zemen, which is the capital town of the *woreda.* The reason is that the sample households live closer to the border of Fogera *woreda* and hence they prefer to visit Woreta, the capital of Fogera *woreda.* Woreta is also bigger than Addis Zemen in terms of providing services.

Table 7.2: Towns visited by households in each *woreda*

Woreda	Towns visited	Percent of visitors
Dembia	Koladiba	78
	Robit	21
Fogera	Woreta	49
	Yefiga	16
	Alamber	15
	Amedber	6
	Asika	6
	Addis Zemen	2
	Waja	2
	Koldiba	1
	Mahkechie	1
Gondar zuria	Teda	99
Libokemkem	Woreta	56
	Yifiga	46
Mecha	Merawi	50
	Arbete	50

SOURCE: Field Data

Table 7.3 shows that the average travel time to towns is one hour and 16 minutes (75.7 minutes), but this varies by *woreda*. Households in Gondar Zuria (48.4 minuses) and Mecha (42.08 minutes) travel less than an hour. The distribution of respondents by travel time shows that half of them travel one hour or less than one hour to visit towns. Out of these, 22% travel less than 30 minutes. These households therefore live close to the towns. A significant proportion (36%), however, lives relatively far and these people have to travel between one and two hours to reach the town. This is particularly so for those households in Dembia (52%) and those in Libokemkem (65%)

Fig 2: Frequency of travel to towns by husband and wives

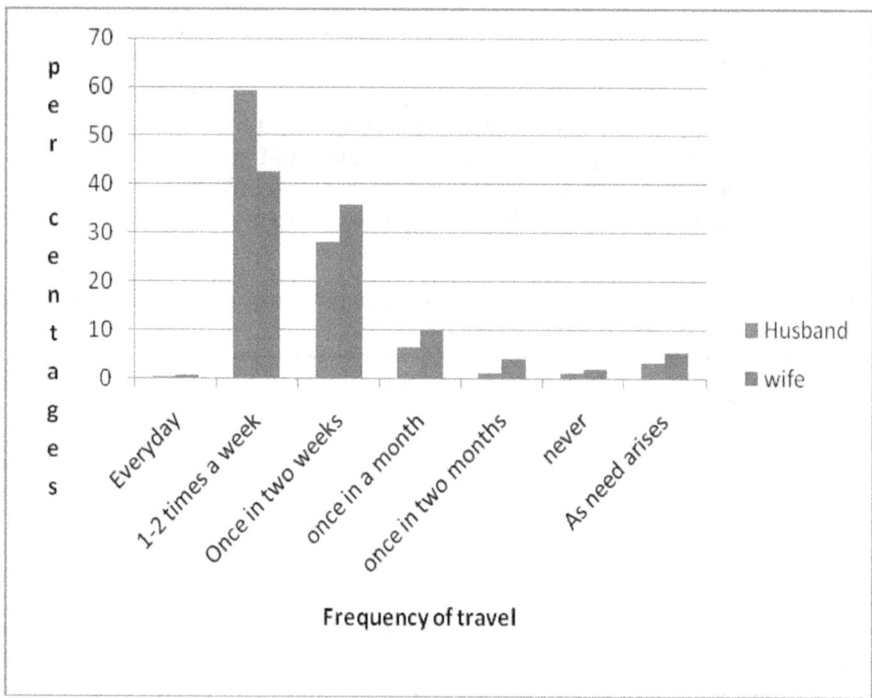

SOURCE: Field Data

Table 7.3 Percentage distribution of respondents by travel times to towns in minutes

Woreda	1.00-30.00	31.00-60.00	61.00-120.00	121.00-180.00	>180.00	Average travel time
Dembia	1.1	32.3	51.6	15.1	-	96.79
Fogera	8.4	33.7	17.9	37.9	2.1	105.02
Gondar Zuria	46.4	24.7	27.8	1.0	-	48.45
Libokemekem	8.2	19.4	65.3	7.1	-	88.28
Mecha	45.5	36.4	18.2	-	-	42.08
Total	22.2	29.3	36.1	12.0	0.4	75.71

SOURCE: Field Data

The overwhelming majority of households (96.3%) travel on foot to towns (Table 7.4). Public transport is not a common mode of transport. It is only 2.5% of the total households who reported the same. In Libokemkem, however, nearly 12% of the households reported the use of public transport .

Table 7.4: Percentage distribution of respondents by travel mode of transport to towns

	On foot	Animal back	Public vehicle	Other
Dembia	100.00	0.0	0.0	0.0
Fogera	99.00	1.0	0.0	0.0
Gondar Zuria	100.00	0.0	0.0	0.0
Libokemekem	85.4	2.1	11.5	0.0
Mecha	96.8	1.1	1.1	1.1
Total	96.3	0.8	2.5	0.2
N	465	4	12	1

SOURCE: Field Data

The main reason to visit towns in the *woredas* covered in this study is to buy and sell items (96.4%). There is no significant *woreda* variation in this regard. The second reason which is visiting health services is cited only by a few respondents (2.1%) though 6% of households in Gondar zuria mentioned the same. Other reasons for visiting towns, such as looking for employment or buying inputs, did not figure as important among the responses. It is therefore easy to understand that rural households go to towns only for marketing purposes. This indicates that rural areas have limited linkage with towns and the existing towns serve only as market centers and not as financial service centers for the surrounding.

Table 7.5: Percentage distribution of respondents by purpose of visit to towns

	Buy and sell items	Look for employment	Buy inputs	Visit health service
Dembia	100.0	0.0	0.0	0.0
Fogera	94.7	0.0	0.0	1.1
Gondar Zuria	93.9	0.0	0.0	6.1
Libokemkem	94.7	0.0	1.1	3.2
Mecha	98.9	1.1	0.0	0.0
Total	96.4	0.2	0.2	2.1
N	451	1	1	10

SOURCE: Field Data

7.2 Non Farm income

Non-farm activities are gaining critical importance in the livelihoods of rural households, particularly in the livelihoods of farmers. It provides alternative sources of income that can support livelihoods and even support the agricultural activity.

Table 7.6 reveals that the proportion of households with non-farm income is about 19%. Mecha *woreda* (44.7%) and Fogera *woreda* (22.3%) have, however, higher proportion of households engaged in non-farm activities. The proportion is lower in Libokemkem (3.1%) and Dembia (10.4%).

Table 7.6: Proportion of households with non-farm income

Woreda	Yes	No
Dembia	10.4	89.6
Fogera	22.3	77.7
Gondar Zuria	17.3	82.7
Libokemkem	3.1	96.9

Mecha	44.7	55.3
Total	19.4	80.6
N (Total)	93	479

SOURCE: Field Data

The diversity of engagement in non-farm activity however is limited. Trade seems to be relatively the most widely practiced non-farm activity particularly in Mecha *woreda* (Table 7.7). Other activities are practiced by less number of households. For instance, local wage income and sales of wood are reported by 18 households each while non-local wage employment is reported by 6 individuals. Mean income is higher for sales of wood followed by local wage employment (Table 7.7). Trade though relatively widely practiced has a lower income compared to wage employment and sales of wood.

With limited engagement in non-farm activity, it remains to be a sector to be developed since it can generate a substantial income to farmers.

Table 7.7 Number of households reporting engagement in different types of activities and their mean income in birr

	Trade		Sales of wood		Local wage employment		Non local wage employment		Handicraft	
Woreda	Number of Participants	Mean income	Number of participants	Mean income	Number of participants	Mean income	Number of participants	mean income	Number of participants	
Dembia	2	1505	2	3250	2	2000	2	2500	1	1800
Fogera	1	1000	7	3843	3	2333	1	200	0	0
Gondar zuria	3	2000	4	1300	6	1280	0	0	0	0
Liboke mkem	1	1300	0	0	0	0	0	0	0	0
Mecha	21	1059	5	1430	7	843	3	600	3	1733
Total	28	1198	18	2542	18	1370	6	900	4	900

SOURCE: Field Data

One of the ways for earning income is by engaging in seasonal migration. Seasonal migration however is not a common phenomenon among households. It is only 5% of the total respondents who reported engagement in seasonal migration. In Gondar Zuria, however, a higher proportion of households (16%)

is engaged in seasonal migration. These households mostly migrate to Humera and Metema. Eight of the sixteen households who reported seasonal migration go to Humera while 2 reported that they migrate to Metema. These places are dotted with large scale commercial farms with an opportunity for seasonal employment.

Table 7.8 Number and percentage of respondents who reported engagement in seasonal migration

Woreda	Frequency	% of total
Dembia	4	4.0
Fogera	2	2.0
Gondar Zuria	16	16
Liobokemkem	0	0
Mecha	1	1
Total	23	4.7

SOURCE: Field Data

7.3 Access to Social services and road

Social services are required by households to meet their different needs. The availability of facilities and services in close proximity is therefore crucial. In Table 7.9, it can be seen that water points (11.04 minutes), primary schools (20 minutes) and health posts (24 minutes) are found in close proximity everywhere. On the other hand, farmers spend long travel time to use telephones (68 minutes), post offices (71 minutes) and reach markets (63 minutes). There is, however, a significant variation between *woredas* with regard to access to services. Mecha *woreda* has a much higher access to services. In this *woreda*, farmers travel only 13 minutes to get access to telephone, five minutes to post office and 22 minutes to reach market centers. In Dembia *Woreda,* on the other hand, farmers are by far further removed from different facilities.

Table 7.9: Average travel time to use the service (minutes)

	Dembia	Fogera	Gondar Zuria	Libokemekem	Mecha	Total
Grain mill	41.98	56.64	41.30	22.62	42.63	40.96
Primary school	16.12	20.12	13.69	31.34	19.03	20.12
Secondary school	18.32	52.83	23.59	60.00	60.00	26.14
Health post	18.30	25.00	17.63	35.57	5.00	24.24
Health center	40.06	48.48	32.33	49.30	22.27	37.16
Veterinary service	86.75	57.19	31.25	49.30	19.96	55.71
Water point	18.90	8.19	9.46	8.71	8.95	11.04
Post office	99.95	55.76	32.15	-	5.00	71.46
Police station	97.35	38.46	16.96	43.22	21.97	46.17
Market center	96.07	82.45	32.21	56.81	21.67	62.66
Telephone communication	102.26	67.06	31.87	48.43	12.50	67.89

SOURCE: Field Data

7.4 Food status and food Aid

Table 7.10 clearly shows that the area studied is generally food secure area in that it is only 10 % of the total households which reported food shortage. Gondar Zuria (30%) is by far the most food insecure area among the *woredas*. In this *woreda*, 15% face food shortage for three months a year while 9% face shortage for two months of a year. However, no one reported food aid in all the *woredas*. This is because the *woredas* do not qualify for food aid assistance by the government.

Table 7.10: Food shortage in a year and number of months of food shortage

			Number of months food shortages occur in a year				Reasons for food shortage		
	Faced food shortage in a year	N	1	2	3	4	Crop failure	Inadequate production	Both crop failure and inadequate production
Dembia**	1.0 (1)	100.0 (98)							1.02 (1)
Fogera	11.3 (11)	100.0 (97)		2.06 (2)	7.21 (7)	(2.06) 2	5.15 (5)	2.06 (2)	4.12 (4)
Gondar Zuria	30.3 (30)	100.0 (99)	2.02 (2)	9.09 (9)	15.15 (15)	4.04 (4)	3.03 (3)	9.09 (9)	11.11 (11)
Libokemkem**	3.1 (3)	100.0 (98)	1.02 (1)		1.02 (1)		1.02 (1)	1.02 (1)	
Mecha**	6.1 (6)	100.0 (99)	2.02 (2)	2.02 (2)			2.02 (2)	2.02 (2)	
Total	10.4 (51)	100.0 (491)							

*figures in parenthesis are number of respondents

** one household from Dembia, one from Libokemkem and two from Mecha did not indicate the number of months they face food shortage.

7.5 Coping strategy for production deficiency

Table 7.10 provides farmers preferred coping strategy in case of production failure. A strategy of selling livestock is the most preferred strategy by 72% of the total households. This strategy is also mentioned by the majority of farmers in all *woredas*. Under such condition, the selling of livestock might entail shortage of oxen during the recovery period. Borrowing (32%) and labor employment (27%) are other preferred strategies of coping with deficiency. Among the different *woredas*, households in Fogera seem to be the ones to resort to diverse means of coping strategies in case of production deficiency. On the other hand, households in Dembia have reported a few strategies limited only to selling of livestock and borrowing.

Table 7.11: Percentage distribution of respondents by preferred coping strategy to deal with production failure*.

Type of coping strategy	Dembia	Fogera	Gondar zuria	Libokemkem	Mecha	Total
Labour employment	1.0	61.9	19.0	32.0	19.0	26.5
Live with shortage	0.0	49.5	5.0	11.0	0.0	13.0
Off-farm work	2.0	51.5	5.0	0.0	2.0	11.9
Selling livestock	74.7	83.5	59.0	92.0	48.5	71.5
Borrowing	42.0	53.6	11.0	31.0	20.2	31.5
Donation	1.0	35.1	0.0	1.0	0.0	7.3
Begging	0.0	4.1	0.0	0.0	2.0	1.2
Migration	0.0	6.3	7.0	21.0	0.0	6.9
Food for work	0.0	18.6	0.0	1.0	0.0	3.8
Sell straw	0.0	29.9	1.0	1.0	0.0	6.3

Farmers provided multiple answers

VIII. POPULATION CHARACTERISTICS OF URBAN HOUSEHOLDS

8.1 Age-Sex Composition

Table 8.1 reveals that there are 1423 members in all the study towns. The males number 642 or 45.1% and the females number 781 or 54.9%. There are thus more females in the study towns with a sex ratio of 82 males for every 100 females. There is significant variation among the towns in sex ratios. Merawi with a sex ratio of 56 males to 100 females have more number of females while Woreta with a sex ratio of 90.5 males to 100 females has more number of males.

The age structure of the total population shows that those below the age of 15 years or those who cannot join the labor force form 35%. The sex distribution of this age group shows that 34 % and 35.4% are males and females respectively. On the other hand, 3.4 % of the household members are above the age of 64. In total therefore those who are not in the productive age group form 38.4% of the total household members. Table 8.2 shows that there is little variation among towns in the age-sex distribution of households.

Table 8.1 Age –sex distribution of total members of households (percent and number)

Age group	Male		Female		Both sex	
	No.	%	No.	%	No.	%
0-4	57	8.9	59	7.6	116	8.2
5-9	71	11.1	101	12.9	172	12.1
10-14	89	13.9	116	14.9	205	14.4
15-19	75	11.7	112	14.3	187	13.1
20-24	67	10.4	73	9.3	140	9.8
25-29	41	6.4	82	10.5	123	8.6
30-34	46	7.2	56	7.2	102	7.2
35-39	45	7.0	64	8.2	109	7.7
40-44	35	5.5	31	4.0	66	4.6
45-49	30	4.7	22	2.8	52	3.7
50-54	28	4.4	23	2.9	51	3.6
55-59	16	2.5	8	1.0	24	1.7
60-64	13	2.0	15	1.9	28	2.0
65-69	16	2.5	9	1.2	25	1.8
70& over	13	2.0	10	1.3	23	1.6
Total	642	100.0	781	100.0	1423	100.0

SOURCE: Field Data

Table 8.2. Age-sex distribution of total members of households by towns (percent and number)

	Dembiya			Fogera			Bahr Dar Zuria			Gondar Zuria			Libo			Mecha			All sample woredas		
Age group	Qoladiba			Woreta			Bahr Dar			Maksegnit			Addis Zemen			Merawi			All sample towns		
	Male (%)	Female (%)	Both sexes	Male (%)	Female (%)	Both sexes	Male (%)	Female (%)	Both sexes	Male (%)	Female (%)	Both sexes	Male (%)	Female (%)	Both sexes	Male (%)	Female (%)	Both sexes	Male (%)	Female (%)	Both sexes
0-4	10.1	10.7	10.4	14.0	12.7	13.3	4.8	2.9	3.8	7.3	11.7	9.7	12.6	6.3	9.0	7.4	5.0	5.8	8.9	7.6	8.2
5 - 9	14.6	12.6	13.5	11.4	17.5	14.6	6.9	7.7	7.3	16.7	14.4	15.5	9.2	17.0	13.6	11.8	12.4	12.2	11.1	12.9	12.1
10 - 14	18.0	14.6	16.1	12.3	10.3	11.3	15.4	14.9	15.2	10.4	12.6	11.6	12.6	15.2	14.1	13.2	21.5	18.5	13.9	14.9	14.4
15-19	7.9	11.7	9.9	13.2	10.3	11.7	13.8	15.9	14.9	6.3	16.2	11.6	13.8	13.4	13.6	13.2	17.4	15.9	11.7	14.3	13.1
20-24	7.9	7.8	7.8	7.9	12.7	10.4	11.2	12.5	11.9	20.8	6.3	13.0	5.7	8.9	7.5	7.4	5.0	5.8	10.4	9.3	9.8
25-29	4.5	9.7	7.3	8.8	12.7	10.8	6.4	9.6	8.1	8.3	9.9	9.2	3.4	10.7	7.5	5.9	10.7	9.0	6.4	10.5	8.6
30-34	9.0	7.8	8.3	8.8	8.7	8.8	5.9	5.8	5.8	4.2	9.9	7.2	8.0	6.3	7.0	8.8	5.8	6.9	7.2	7.2	7.2
35-39	9.0	8.7	8.9	7.9	4.8	6.3	4.3	10.1	7.3	10.4	5.4	7.7	6.9	8.9	8.0	5.9	9.9	8.5	7.0	8.2	7.7
40-44	4.5	3.9	4.2	4.4	2.4	3.3	6.4	4.3	5.3	3.1	2.7	2.9	5.7	5.4	5.5	8.8	5.0	6.3	5.5	4.0	4.6
45-49	3.4	1.9	2.6	2.6	2.4	2.5	4.8	4.8	4.8	3.1	2.7	2.9	6.9	0.9	3.5	8.8	2.5	4.8	4.7	2.8	3.7

50-54	4.5	3.9	4.2	1.8	1.6	1.7	6.4	2.4	4.3	3.1	4.5	3.9	4.6	3.6	4.0	4.4	2.5	3.2	4.4	2.9	3.6
55-59	2.2	1.9	2.1	2.6	0.0	1.3	2.1	1.4	1.8	2.1	0.9	1.4	2.3	0.9	1.5	4.4	0.8	2.1	2.5	1.0	1.7
60-64	0.0	1.0	0.5	1.8	1.6	1.7	3.2	3.8	3.5	1.0	0.9	1.0	4.6	0.9	2.5	0.0	1.7	1.1	2.0	1.9	2.0
65-69	3.4	1.0	2.1	1.8	0.8	1.3	3.2	2.4	2.8	2.1	0.9	1.4	3.4	0.9	2.0	0.0	0.0	0.0	2.5	1.2	1.8
70& over	1.1	2.9	2.1	0.9	1.6	1.3	5.3	1.4	3.3	1.0	0.9	1.0	0.0	0.9	0.5	0.0	0.0	0.0	2.0	1.3	1.6
Total (No)	89	103	192	114	126	240	188	208	396	96	111	207	87	112	199	68	121	189	642	781	142 3
Age Sex Ratio			86.4			90.5			90.4			86.5			77.7			56.2			82.2

SOURCE: Field Data

The age dependency ratio which is the ratio of non-productive persons (persons aged 0 to 14 and 65 and over) to productive persons (persons aged 15 to 64) was estimated on the basis of a broader age group distribution (Table 8.3). Accordingly, the overall dependency ratio is 61% or 0.6 which implies that there are nearly two dependent persons for one non-dependent person. The highest dependency ratio is registered in Qoladiba where the dependency ratio reached 79%. This is because there is a higher young dependency ratio in the town. The highest old dependency ratio is registered for Bahr Dar Zuria with a ratio reaching 9%. Though the dependency ratios in towns are not as high as in rural areas, there is still a high level of dependency in all towns.

Table 8.3 Distribution of persons by broad age group and dependency ratio

		Age group			**Dependency ratio**		
Woreda	**Town**	**<15 years**	**15-64 years**	**65 & above**	**young**	**Old**	**total**
Dembiya	Qoladiba	40.1	55.7	4.2	71.9	7.5	79.4
Fogera	Woreta	39.2	58.3	2.5	67.2	4.2	71.4
Bahr Dar Zuria	Bahr Dar	26.3	67.7	6.1	38.8	9.0	47.8
Gondar Zuria	Maksegnit	36.7	60.9	2.4	60.4	3.9	64.3
Libo	Addis Zemen	36.7	60.8	2.5	60.4	4.1	64.5
Mecha	Merawi	36.5	63.5	0.0	57.4	0.0	57.4
Total	**34.6**	**61.9**	**3.4**	**55.8**	**5.4**	**61.2**	

SOURCE: Field Data

8.2. Household Composition and Marital Status

Table 8.4 shows the household headship and household size in the study towns. The towns show that a significant proportion of households (32%) is female headed households. At this point it might be said that gender oriented intervention may be relevant in the study towns. The table also reveals that town variation is significant in terms of types of headship. Woreta with 88% of households headed by males and only 10% by females is dominated by male headship while Merawi with 40% female headed households has a higher proportion of female headed households.

Table 8.4 Percentage distribution of households by sex of household head, household size and place of residence

			Household Headship		Household Size						
Woreda	**Town**	**All HHs**	**% Male Head**	**% Female Head**	**1**	**2**	**3**	**4**	**5**	**6 & above**	**Average**
Dembiya	Qoladiba	50	64.0	36.0	6.0	14.0	20.0	22.0	20.0	16.0	3.9
Fogera	Woreta	50	88.0	10.0	2.0	6.0	8.0	24.0	22.0	36.0	4.9
Bahr Dar Zuria	Bahr Dar	100	67.0	33.0	9.0	15.0	16.0	15.0	27.0	18.0	4.0
Gondar Zuria	Maksegnit	50	62.0	38.0	8.0	10.0	14.0	32.0	12.0	24.0	4.3
Libo	Addis Zemen	50	66.0	34.0	4.0	16.0	18.0	24.0	22.0	16.0	4.0
Mecha	Merawi	50	60.0	40.0	8.0	22.0	10.0	24.0	24.0	12.0	3.8
Total (All sample towns)		350	67.7	32.0	6.6	14.0	14.6	22.3	22.0	**20.0**	**4.2**

SOURCE: Field Data

The average household size in all towns is 4.2 (table 8.4) and this is less than the average household for rural areas of the surrounding which was reported to be 5.3 (see the rural section). The smallest household size is found in Merawi with 3.8 and the highest is in Woreta with 4.9 or nearly 5 persons per household. In terms of household members, 42% of the households have 5 or more members. Families with 3 or less members constitute 35% of the households. This just shows the distribution of households is skewed towards a higher family size.

The sample households are dominated by married households (67%) (Table 8.5). Singles are only 6% while 27% are no more living in union though they were once married. The latter groups are divorced (17%), separated (7%) or widowed (3%). A closer look at the towns reveals that Woreta (90%) has the highest married couples while it is only half (50%) in Merawi which belong to this group. In the same way, Merawi and Qoladiba have the highest proportion of couples not living in union.

Table 8.5: Percentage of households by marital status of household heads by towns

Woreda	Town	All HHs	Single (%)	Married (%)	Divorced (%)	Separated (%)	Widowed (%)
Dembiya	Qoladiba	50	2.0	62.0	26.0	6.0	2.0
Fogera	Woreta	50	0.0	90.0	4.0	2.0	2.0
Bahr Dar Zuria	Bahr Dar	100	11.0	64.0	13.0	11.0	0.0
Gondar Zuria	Maksegnit	50	0.0	68.0	18.0	8.0	6.0
Libo	Addis Zemen	50	2.0	68.0	22.0	4.0	4.0
Mecha	Merawi	50	14.0	50.0	24.0	8.0	4.0
Total (All sample towns)		350	5.7	66.6	17.1	7.1	2.6

SOURCE: Field Data

8.3 Ethnic and Religious Composition

Table 8.6 shows that Amhara and Orthodox are the main ethnic and religious groups respectively. Households in the study towns are therefore polarized in terms of their religious and ethnic characteristics.

Table 8.6: Percentage of households by ethnic and religious group

			Ethnic group		Religion		
Woreda	Town	All HHs	Amhara (%)	Tigray (%)	Orthodox (%)	Islam (%)	Protestant (%)
Dembiya	Qoladiba	50	96.0	2.0	82.0	16.0	0.0
Fogera	Woreta	50	96.0	2.0	98.0	0.0	0.0
Bahr Dar	Bahr Dar	100	94.0	5.0	89.0	7.0	4.0
G/Zuria	Maksegnit	50	100.0	0.0	72.0	28.0	0.0
Libo	Addis Zemen	50	100.0	0.0	96.0	4.0	0.0
Mecha	Merawi	50	98.0	0.0	98.0	2.0	0.0
Total (All sample towns)		350	96.9	2.0	89.1	9.1	1.1

SOURCE: Field Data

8.4 Educational characteristics

Table 8.7 shows that a slightly more than one-fifth of the population (23.4%) is illiterate. The illiterates are much higher in Woreta (37%), Addis Zemen (36%) and Maksegnit (28%). Such a significant proportion indicates that many people are not benefiting from education. With regard to formal education, those who have completed primary education (21.6%) are of the same proportion as those who completed high school (22%).

Educational status by sex shows that females (35%) are more illiterate than males (24%) (Table 8.8). Illiterate females are much more in number in Maksegnit (45%) and Woreta (48%). On the other hand 62% of males have attained primary level or above educational characteristic while females in this category are 55%. The fact that females are more illiterate than males indicates that there has to be educational program that focuses on women to improve their levels of literacy.

8.5 Primary Activity

Table 8.9 shows that 59% of the total population is not currently part of the active labor force. This group is composed of children (4.1%), students (42%) and housewives (13%). Among those who are currently active in the labor force, 15% reported that they are self-employed while 12% are employed either by government/parastatal organization (7.8%) or private sector (4.1%). Among the study towns, self-employed people are higher in Qoladiba (21%), Maksegnit (25%), and Addis Zemen (26%) while relatively more government employees are witnessed in Merawi (14%). Though all the towns belong to small towns and lower middle towns, there are only a few people engaged in farming (5%) though a significant proportion of town's people in Woreta (18%) eke their living from farming. There are more male government employees, private sector employee and self-employed.(Table 8.10)

Table 8.7: Percentage distribution of members of respondent hhs by Educational status.

Woreda	Town	No of respondents aged 6 years and above	% None	% Read only	% Read & write only	% Kinder garten	% Primary	% Junior sec.	% Seconda ry	% Diploma	% Degree
Dembiya	Qoladiba	169	18.9	2.4	4.7	3.0	25.4	13.0	27.8	3.6	1.2
Fogera	Woreta	202	36.6	1.0	14.4	0.5	22.8	0.0	15.8	6.9	1.5
Bahr Dar Zuria	Bahr Dar	374	12.6	1.3	3.7	0.8	17.1	23.5	27.3	8.6	5.1
Gondar Zuria	Maksegnit	183	27.9	5.5	11.5	4.4	19.7	8.2	19.1	2.7	1.1
Libo	Addis Zemen	177	35.6	1.7	11.3	0.0	26.6	1.7	16.9	3.4	2.8
Mecha	Merawi	171	18.7	3.5	2.9	3.5	22.8	14.0	20.5	9.4	4.7
Total (All sample towns)		1276	23.4	2.4	7.6	1.8	21.6	11.9	22.0	6.2	3.1

SOURCE: field data

Table 8.8: Percentage of household members by education, sex and town

	Dembiya		Fogera		Bahr Dar Zuria		Gondar Zuria		Libo		Mecha		All sample woredas	
Education level	**Qoladiba**		**Woreta**		**Bahr Dar**		**Maksegnit**		**Addis Zemen**		**Merawi**		**All sample towns**	
	Male (%)	Female (%)	Male (%)	Female (%)	Male (%)	Female (%)	Male (%)	Female (%)	Male (%)	Female (%)	Male (%)	Female (%)	Male (%)	Female (%)
None	20.2	35.0	43.0	48.4	10.6	20.7	25.0	44.6	37.9	44.6	13.2	26.4	23.8	34.7
Read only	2.2	1.9	0.9	0.8	0.5	1.9	4.2	6.3	3.4	0.0	2.9	3.3	2.0	2.3
Read and write only	5.6	2.9	17.5	7.3	3.2	4.3	11.5	8.9	12.6	8.0	4.4	2.5	8.7	5.5
Kindergarten	4.5	1.9	0.0	2.4	3.2	1.4	5.2	2.7	0.0	1.8	8.8	6.6	3.3	2.7
Primary	21.3	23.3	20.2	18.5	14.4	17.8	19.8	15.2	21.8	25.0	13.2	24.8	18.1	20.4
Junior sec.	12.4	10.7	0.0	0.0	27.1	17.8	5.2	8.9	0.0	2.7	14.7	11.6	12.0	9.6
Secondary	27.0	22.3	9.6	16.9	26.6	24.5	25.0	10.7	16.1	14.3	22.1	16.5	21.5	18.3
Diploma	5.6	1.0	7.0	4.8	8.0	8.2	3.1	1.8	2.3	3.6	11.8	6.6	6.4	4.9
Degree	1.1	1.0	1.8	0.8	6.4	3.4	1.0	0.9	5.7	0.0	8.8	1.7	4.2	1.5
Total (N)	89	103	114	124	188	208	96	112	87	112	68	121	642	780

SOURCE: Field Data

Table 8.9: Distribution of household members aged 7 and above by occupation and town

Woreda	**Town**	**All respondents aged > 7**	**% Child**	**% School**	**% House wife**	**% Gov./ Parastatal employee**	**% Private sector employee**	**% Self - employe d**	**% Farme r**	**% Other**
Dembiya	Qoladiba	161	3.1	43.5	18.0	5.0	4.3	21.1	1.2	3.7
Fogera	Woreta	194	6.7	37.6	18.0	6.7	3.1	5.2	17.5	5.2
Bahr Dar Zuria	Bahr Dar	369	1.4	41.7	9.8	9.2	6.2	8.9	2.2	20.6
Gondar Zuria	Maksegnit	177	5.6	46.9	10.2	3.4	1.1	25.4	2.3	5.1
Libo	Addis Zemen	168	5.4	39.9	13.1	6.5	0.6	26.2	2.4	6.0
Mecha	Merawi	167	5.4	41.9	11.4	14.4	7.2	12.6	4.8	2.4
Total (All sample towns)		1236	4.1	41.8	12.9	7.8	4.1	15.1	4.9	9.3

SOURCE: Field Data

Table 8:10: Percentage of household members by occupation, sex and town

	Dembiya		Fogera		Bahr Dar Zuria		Gondar Zuria		Libo		Mecha		All sample woredas	
Occupation/ Activity	**Qoladiba**		**Woreta**		**Bahr Dar**		**Maksegnit**		**Addis Zemen**		**Merawi**		**All sample towns**	
	Male (%)	Female (%)	Male (%)	Female (%)	Male (%)	Female (%)	Male (%)	Female (%)	Male (%)	Female (%)	Male (%)	Female (%)	Male (%)	Female (%)
Child	14.6	15.5	23.9	22.0	5.3	5.4	11.5	20.5	19.5	17.9	8.8	12.4	13.1	14.4
School	42.7	37.9	29.2	33.3	44.4	38.0	47.9	38.4	33.3	36.6	36.8	45.5	39.7	38.3
House wife	0.0	28.2	1.8	26.8	1.1	16.6	2.1	15.2	0.0	19.6	0.0	15.7	0.9	19.8
Government /parastatal employee	6.7	1.9	8.0	3.3	12.3	5.4	4.2	1.8	8.0	3.6	26.5	5.0	10.5	3.7
Private sector employee	5.6	1.9	5.3	0.0	7.0	4.9	1.0	0.9	1.1	0.0	10.3	4.1	5.2	2.3
Self employed	24.7	11.7	5.3	3.3	10.7	6.3	26.0	17.9	26.4	18.8	7.4	13.2	15.8	11.1
Farmer	2.2	0.0	23.9	5.7	2.7	1.5	3.1	0.9	4.6	0.0	10.3	0.8	7.5	1.5
Other	3.4	2.9	2.7	5.7	16.6	22.0	4.2	4.5	6.9	3.6	0.0	3.3	7.3	8.8
Total (N)	89	103	113	123	187	205	96	112	87	112	68	121	640	776

SOURCE: Field Data

IX. MIGRATION STATUS

9.1 Incident of migration and work in previous location

Table 9.1 shows that migrants form 56% of the total households. There is however some variation among towns. Bigger towns such as Bahr Dar (63%), Maksegnit (62%) and Merawi (76%) have more migrants compared with Addis Zemen (40%) and Qoladiba (43%) and Woreta (41%). It can also be seen that 39% of the spouses are migrants. Bahr Dar (54%), Woreta (44%) and Merawi (43%) have more number of migrant spouses.

Table 9.1: Migration status of household head and principal spouse

		Household head				Principal spouse		
Woreda	**Town**	**Total sample household**	**HH heads who responded**	**Not moved (%)**	**Moved (%)**	**Principal spouse who responded**	**not moved (%)**	**moved (%)**
Dembiya	Qoladiba	50	49	57.1	42.8	49	77.6	22.4
Fogera	Woreta	50	49	59.1	40.8	48	56.3	43.8
Bahr Dar G/Zuria	Bahr Dar	100	100	37.0	63.0	86	46.5	53.5
	Maksegnit	50	50	38.0	62.0	44	75.0	25.0
Libo	Addis Zemen	50	50	60.0	40.0	49	67.3	32.7
Mecha	Merawi	50	50	24.0	76.0	42	57.1	42.9
Total (All sample towns)		350	348	44.5	55.5	318	61.3	38.7

SOURCE: field data

Table 9.2 shows that 51.1% of the migrant household heads were farmers and 9.5% were herders in their previous locations. These two occupations together form 60.5% and originate in rural areas. This indicates that rural urban migration dominates the migration scenes in the area. In fact in other towns such as Woreta (75%), Libo Kemkem (75%), Maksegnit (65%), Merawi (74%), migrants with farming and herding background are significantly higher implying the importance of rural urban migration in these towns. In contrary to this, migrants to Bahr Dar with farming and herding background account only for 44%. This might indicate that migrants with rural origin are less in number in Bahr Dar than those in small towns. The previous occupation of spouses is dominated by farming (39.8) and herding (11%) implying that spouses mainly originate from rural areas as well (table 9.3).

9.2 Reasons for migration

The major reason for moving to the town is search for jobs (47%) followed by trading or the need to undertake business (16%) (Table 9.4). The two reasons together account for 63% of the respondents and signify the importance of economic reason as the major motivation for the migration of household heads. Social reasons (13%) and education (8.4%) form other major reason for migration. The responses in different towns correspond with the responses of the total sample except for Merawi where job search and business each accounted only for 11% and while social reasons accounted for 37% and education accounted for 21 %.

With regard to spouses, the most important reason for migration is marriage (33.1%) (Table 9.5). It appears therefore that non-economic reason drives women to migrate to towns. Economic reason however is also significant in that nearly 28% of the respondents migrated for purposes of taking up jobs (table 9.5).

9.3 Duration of migration

Tables 9.6 and 9.7 reveal that migrant households and migrant spouses in different towns are relatively long term migrants. Short-term migrants who lived in the town for less than 6 years constitute 22% of the household heads and 19% of their spouses. Migrant household heads on average have lived for 17 years in the towns and migrant spouses have lived in the town for an average of 16 years. The fact that most are long term migrants may indicate that migrants are well adapted to the circumstances in the towns. It also reveals migrants once they moved to woreda capitals prefer to stay there for long period instead of continuing with their migration and moving to other towns.

Table 9.2: Percentage distribution of migrant household head by previous occupation and by town

Woreda	Town	Migrant hh heads	% farming	% herding	% wage employment	% Casual work	% government employee	% Military /police	% trading /selling	% other
Dembiya	Qoladiba	21	30.0	19.0	0.0	0.0	0.0	9.5	23.8	19.0
Fogera	Woreta	20	65.0	10.0	5.0	0.0	0.0	5.0	0.0	15.0
Bahr Dar Zuria	Bahr Dar	60	26.7	16.7	3.3	1.7	11.7	6.7	6.7	26.7
Gondar Zuria	Maksegnit	31	67.7	0.0	0.0	0.0	0.0	0.0	3.2	29.0
Libo	Addis Zemen	20	65.0	10.0	0.0	0.0	0.0	10.0	10.0	5.0
Mecha	Merawi	38	73.7	0.0	0.0	0.0	0.0	0.0	5.3	21.1
Total (All sample towns)		190	51.1	9.5	1.6	0.5	3.7	4.7	7.4	21.6

SOURCE: field data

Table 9.3: Percentage distribution of migrant spouses by previous occupation and town

Woreda	Town	All HHs	Responding migrant spouses	Farming (%)	Herding (%)	wage employment (%)	Casual Work (%)	Government employee (%)	Military /police (%)	Trading /selling (%)	other (%)
Dembiya	Qoladiba	50	8	0.0	0.0	0.0	0.0	0.0	0.0	0.0	100.0
Fogera	Woreta	50	21	47.6	19.0	0.0	0.0	0.0	0.0	9.5	23.8
Bahr Dar	Bahr Dar	100	44	15.9	18.2	2.3	0.0	4.5	2.3	2.3	54.5
G/Zuria	Maksegnit	50	11	54.5	0.0	0.0	0.0	9.1	0.0	0.0	36.4

Libo	Addis Zemen	50	16	68.8	6.3	0.0	0.0	0.0	0.0	0.0	25.0
Mecha	Merawi	50	18	72.2	0.0	0.0	0.0	0.0	0.0	0.0	27.8
Total (All sample towns)		350	118	39.8	11.0	0.8	0.0	2.5	0.8	2.5	42.4

SOURCE: field data

Table 9.4: Percentage distribution of migrant household heads by reasons for migration and towns.

Woreda	**Town**	**Migrant HHs**	**Take up job (%)**	**Trading/ Business (%)**	**Social reasons (%)**	**Education (%)**	**Forced by drought (%)**	**Resettlement program**	**Obtained plot here (%)**	**Live near family (%)**	**Marriage (%)**	**Divorce (%)**	**Live near services (%)**	**Others (%)**
Dembiya	Qoladiba	21	52.4	19.0	4.8	14.3	0.0	0.0	0.0	0.0	9.5	0.0	0.0	0.0
Fogera	Woreta	18	50.0	22.2	5.6	11.1	0.0	5.6	0.0	0.0	5.6	0.0	0.0	0.0
Bahr Dar G/Zuria	Bahr Dar	62	67.7	9.7	1.6	4.8	0.0	0.0	0.0	4.8	1.6	3.2	4.8	1.6
	Maksegnit	31	35.5	25.8	19.4	0.0	0.0	3.2	3.2	3.2	0.0	3.2	0.0	6.5
Libo	Addis Zemen	20	60.0	20.0	5.0	0.0	0.0	0.0	0.0	5.0	10.0	0.0	0.0	0.0
Mecha	Merawi	38	10.5	10.5	36.8	21.1	2.6	2.6	0.0	2.6	7.9	0.0	2.6	2.6
Total (All sample towns)		190	46.8	15.8	12.6	8.4	0.5	1.6	0.5	3.2	4.7	1.6	2.1	2.1

Table 9.5: Percentage distribution of migrant spouses by reasons for migration and towns.

Woreda	Town	Responding migrant spouses	% Take up job	% Trading /business	% Social reasons	% Education	% Resettlement program	% Live near family	% Marriage	% Divorce	% Live near services
Dembiya	Qoladiba	11	9.1	0.0	18.2	27.3	0.0	0.0	45.5	0.0	0.0
Fogera	Woreta	17	29.4	5.9	0.0	0.0	5.9	23.5	35.3	0.0	0.0
Bahr Dar	Bahr Dar	45	37.8	8.9	0.0	2.2	2.2	8.9	33.3	0.0	6.7
G/Zuria	Maksegnit	11	9.1	9.1	18.2	0.0	0.0	18.2	36.4	9.1	0.0
Libo	Addis Zemen	16	50.0	18.8	12.5	0.0	0.0	0.0	18.8	0.0	0.0
Mecha	Merawi	18	5.6	16.7	11.1	22.2	5.6	5.6	33.3	0.0	0.0
Total (All sample towns)		118	28.0	10.2	6.8	6.8	2.5	9.3	33.1	0.8	2.5

SOURCE: field data

Table 9.6: Number of years migrant household head lived in towns (percentage)

Woreda	Town	Number of HHs with migrant HH head	1 -3 years	4 - 6 years	7 - 10 years	11 - 15 years	16 - 20 years	> = 21 years	Average Years lived
Dembiya	Qoladiba	21	4.8	14.3	19.0	9.5	14.3	38.1	18.2
Fogera	Woreta	16	18.8	6.3	25.0	37.5	0.0	12.5	13.1

Bahr Dar	Bahr Dar	60	6.7	15.0	10.0	10.0	15.0	43.3	21.4
G/Zuria	Maksegnit	29	13.8	13.8	6.9	10.3	13.8	41.4	18.6
Libo	Addis Zemen	19	5.3	5.3	15.8	21.1	5.3	47.4	17.3
Mecha	Merawi	38	10.5	13.2	21.1	18.4	15.8	21.1	14.8
Total (All sample towns)		183	9.3	12.6	14.8	15.3	12.6	35.5	17.2

SOURCE: field data

Table 9.7: Number of years migrant spouses lived in the town (Percentage)

Woreda	Town	Number of all migrant spouse	1 - 3 years	4 - 6 years	7- 10 years	11 -15 years	% 16 - 20 years	>= 21 years	Average Years lived
Dembiya	Qoladiba	11	0.0	9.1	9.1	27.3	18.2	36.4	20.9
Fogera	Woreta	16	12.5	12.5	25.0	37.5	6.3	6.3	11.2
Bahr Dar Zuria	Bahr Dar	43	4.7	11.6	14.0	16.3	20.9	32.6	18.0
Gondar Zuria	Maksegnit	8	25.0	12.5	0.0	37.5	0.0	25.0	15.5
Libo	Addis Zemen	15	13.3	0.0	13.3	40.0	6.7	26.7	16.2
Mecha	Merawi	17	11.8	11.8	11.8	35.3	17.6	11.8	13.0
Total (All sample towns)	110	9.1	10.0	13.6	28.2	14.5	24.5	15.8	

SOURCE: field data

X. EMPLOYMENT, INCOME AND ENGAGEMENT IN BUSINESS

10.1 Types of employment and working status of household members

The major form of employment among all samples is business/trading/selling where 29% is engaged in this activity (table 10.1). Wage employment is also significant in that both private and government wage employment together account for 25% of the households. The proportion of households employed both in private and government organizations are split equally into two. Farming is taken up by 11% of the household. Farming, however, is dominated in Woreta where 46% of the household head reported to be engaged in farming. The possible reason could be that Woreta is one of the towns that have irrigation potential in the surrounding areas forcing urban dwellers to engage in rental farming practices.

The working status of household members aged 10 years and above is shown in table 10.2 About 57% of all households mentioned that they have household members who are not currently working. Households with not working members reached 75% in Bahr Dar and 66% in Merawi. Household members with no work are mostly students (44%). About 5% however indicated they are not working mainly because there is no work for them. In Bahr Dar however those with no work because they could not get jobs reached 13%. This is an indication of the fact that in big towns more number of people are not working due to lack of employment opportunities.

10.2 Household income

The monthly income of respondents is shown in table 10.3. It can be seen that the average monthly income from all sources is 2213 birr. This income varies significantly by towns. Respondents in Bahr Dar receive the highest monthly income (4161 birr). The second average monthly income is in Woreta town with 2546 birr. The lowest monthly income is recorded in Qoladiba (983 birr). It appears that households in big towns receive higher income compared to those in small towns. Wage earnings (1754 birr) and earnings from farms (1610 birr) are the highest earnings or income of households. On the other hand pension income (359 birr) and earning from livestock (536 birr) yield the lowest amount of income. Business brings an average income of birr 1200 which is less than both wage earning and farm income. The reason for such low business income could be due to the nature of the business types which are conducted in the study towns.

Table 10.1: Percentage distribution of household head by employment type and town

Woreda	Town	All HHs	Wage employee private	Wage employee government	business/trading /selling	farming	Pension	Other	No answer
Dembiya	Qoladiba	50	22.0	14.0	50.0	2.0	2.0	2.0	8.0
Fogera	Woreta	50	6.0	14.0	22.0	46.0	2.0	2.0	8.0
Bahr Dar G/Zuria	Bahr Dar	100	17.0	23.0	32.0	3.0	8.0	13.0	4.0
	Maksegnit	50	18.0	8.0	36.0	6.0	0.0	30.0	2.0
Libo	Addis Zemen	50	6.0	14.0	30.0	6.0	6.0	30.0	8.0
Mecha	Merawi	50	40.0	24.0	2.0	8.0	0.0	26.0	0.0
Total (All sample towns)		350	18.0	17.1	29.1	10.6	3.7	16.6	4.9

SOURCE: Field Data

Table 10.2: Working status of household members with 10 years and above and reasons for not working

		Work status of household members with 10 years and above				% households with reasons for not working					
Woreda	Town	All HHs	Not working	Working	No answer	Looking after house & family	Sick	too old/ retired	No work	Student/ attending school	No answer
Dembiya	Qoladiba	50	32.0	66.0	2.0	14.0	2.0	0.0	0.0	14.0	2.0
Fogera	Woreta	50	38.0	54.0	8.0	2.0	0.0	2.0	2.0	30.0	2.0
Bahr Dar G/Zuria	Bahr Dar	100	75.0	23.0	2.0	3.0	1.0	3.0	13.0	55.0	0.0
	Maksegnit	50	58.0	42.0	0.0	2.0	0.0	0.0	4.0	44.0	8.0
Libo	Addis Zemen	50	52.0	48.0	0.0	0.0	0.0	0.0	2.0	46.0	4.0

Mecha	Merawi	50	66.0	34.0	0.0	0.0	0.0	2.0	0.0	64.0	0.0
Total (All sample towns)		350	56.6	41.4	2.0	3.4	0.6	1.4	4.9	44.0	2.3

SOURCE: Field Data

Table 10.3: Percent distribution of households who reported income by income sources

		Wage		Business income		Remittance		Farm income		Livestock income		Pension		Others		Total	
Town	**All HHs**	**% hhs**	**Mean income**	**% hhs**	**Mean income**	**% hhs**	**Mean income**	**% hhs**	**Mean income**	**% hhs**	**Mean income**	**% hhs**	**Mean income**	**% hhs**	**Mean income**	**% hhs**	**Mean income**
Qoladiba	50	34.0	827.1	56.0	962.9	8.0	925.0	4.0	903.0	0.0	0.0	2.0	300.0	0.0	0.0	92.0	983.2
Woreta	50	28.0	1374.1	38.0	1161.6	2.0	1000.0	68.0	1754.4	32.0	488.8	8.0	308.8	6.0	427.7	96.0	2545.9
Bahr Dar	100	50.0	2072.7	43.0	2263.5	19.0	2288.5	5.0	3120.2	7.0	1157.1	13.0	299.8	5.0	1280.2	87.0	4161.7
Maksegnit	50	18.0	1493.6	58.0	829.8	20.0	675.0	10.0	1000.0	6.0	233.3	4.0	600.0	36.0	368.9	98.0	1136.6
Addis Zemen	50	26.0	1807.2	70.0	504.3	14.0	500.0	14.0	471.4	18.0	262.2	10.0	271.4	32.0	440.0	98.0	1098.7
Merawi	50	44.0	2062.7	22.0	1504.5	0.0	0.0	10.0	1616.4	2.0	300.0	4.0	847.0	30.0	1022.0	100.0	1781.3
Total all Sample towns	350	35.7	1754	47.1	1240.2	11.7	1425.1	16.6	1611.0	10.3	535.6	7.7	358.6	16.3	643.8	94.0	2213.0

SOURCE: Field Data

10.3 Business types and trends in business engagement

Table 10.4 shows the business types in all the study towns and in each town. The most important business type in all study towns is retail trade which includes grain trade, and selling of different items (35%). The second most important business type is selling of local alcohols (araki and tella) and running of small cafes and hotels (31%). Handicraft which includes tailoring, plumbing, woodwork, metalwork (11%) forms the third important business types in all the study towns. These are in general low paying businesses which do not yield much income. Under the other category, people reported activities such as guarding etc as their main activity though this cannot be included as business types.

Businesses in the study towns hire very few people. For example it is only 53 business people who reported that they hire labor in their businesses. The average number of employees in each business is 1.7 or nearly 2 persons. This is then an indication that businesses in the locality are run by the owners with little employment opportunity for others.

Table 10.4: Business types in study towns

Woreda	Town	Reporting house holds	Retail trade	Hand Craft work	Local alcohol selling, cafes and hotels	Daily laborer	other
Dembiya	Qoladiba	28	28.5	17.8	32.1	7.1	14.2
Fogera	Woreta	9	55.5	0	11.1	11.1	22.2
Bahr Dar Zuria	Bair Dar	30	66.6	16.6	10	3.3	3.3
Gondar Zuria	Makisagite	19	36.8	10.5	31.5	10.5	10.5
Libo	Addis Zemen	20	10	10	50	20	10
Mecha	Merawi	18	11.1	0	55.5	11.1	22.2
Total		124	35.4	11.2	31.4	9.6	12.0

SOURCE: Field Data

Table 10.5 shows the location of the business run by the household. Most household heads (48%) run their businesses in house. This is quite understandable since a significant proportion of the businesses include selling homemade beverages which is usually done from one's own house. It then appears that houses are not only places to live but also sources of income. A significant proportion (26%) also uses the market area as their location of business. Those who use variable location are only 10% while others use fixed locations

Table 10.5: Location of businesses operated by household heads

			Location of the business operated by the HH heads				
Woreda	**Town**	**Reporting hhs**	**% in house /on plot**	**% fixed location**	**% market area**	**% variable location**	**% other**
Dembiya	Qoladiba	36	47.2	25.0	16.7	11.1	0.0
Fogera	Woreta	15	13.3	0.0	86.7	0.0	0.0
Bahr Dar G/Zuria	Bahr Dar	36	33.3	25.0	30.6	11.1	0.0
	Maksegnit	29	51.7	13.8	27.6	6.9	0.0
Libo	Addis Zemen	21	52.4	9.5	19.0	14.3	4.8
Mecha	Merawi	26	80.8	7.7	0.0	11.5	0.0
Total (All sample towns)		**163**	**47.9**	**16.0**	**25.8**	**9.8**	**0.6**

SOURCE: Field Data

Table 10.6: Sales and trends in business income

					Trends in business income		
Woreda	**Town**	**Number of reporting households**	**Average monthly sales revenue from the last period of accounts (birr)**	**Number of Reporting households**	**increased (%)**	**Decreased (%)**	**Remain the same**
Dembiya	Qoladiba	28	1410	24	4.2	45.8	50.0
Fogera	Woreta	18	784.4	16	0.0	81.3	18.8
Bahr Dar G/Zuria	Bahr Dar	26	2116.5	36	25.0	25.0	50.0
	Maksegnit	27	869.8	29	0.0	93.1	6.9
Libo	Addis Zemen	23	907.3	28	0.0	78.6	21.4
Mecha	Merawi	24	1659.8	24	8.3	83.3	8.3
Total (All sample towns)		**146**	**1320.6**	**157**	**7.6**	**65.0**	**27.4**

SOURCE: Field Data

Table 10.6 shows monthly sales and trends in business income. The average monthly sale for all businesses in all towns is 1321 birr. Monthly sales are higher in Bahr Dar town with an average of 2116 birr. Since the reported amount is total sales, it appears that the profit business men get in the study town is very limited. With regard to trends in income, a significant proportion (65%) indicated that business income in the last 12 months has declined while 27% mentioned that business income has not changed. It is only 8% who reported that business income has increased. Since the majority has stated that income has either declined or remained the same, businesses in the study towns therefore are not growing.

The most important use of earnings from business is for household expense (table 10.7). About 71% of the reporting household heads have indicated that they use the business income for household item. About 11% use the business income for asset accumulation particularly for buying houses. It is only 8% of the reporting households who mentioned that earnings from business could be used for investment and running businesses. To the extent that most households use business income for consumption, the use of earnings for business growth is very limited.

Table 10.7: Use of earnings from business by towns

			Primary purpose of the business operated by the HH heads				
Woreda	**Town**	**Number of Reporting households**	**House hold Expense (%)**	**Education and health (%)**	**Asserts and House purchase (%)**	**Saving and running business (%)**	**Other (%)**
Dembiya	Qoladiba	33	81.8	0.0	0.0	0.0	18.2
Fogera	Woreta	14	7.1	0.0	78.6	14.3	0.0
Bahr Dar	Bahr Dar	32	81.3	9.4	0.0	9.4	0.0
G/Zuria	Maksegnit	19	68.4	0.0	10.5	10.5	10.5
Libo	Addis Zemen	22	63.6	0.0	9.1	18.2	9.1
Mecha	Merawi	23	91.3	0.0	4.3	4.3	0.0
Total (All sample towns)		143	71.3	2.1	11.2	8.4	7.0

SOURCE: Field Data

XI. ACCESS TO AND UTILIZATION OF SERVICES

11.1. Access to Services

The baseline study has attempted to examine the state of in regard to accessing various kinds of amenities in terms of heath, veterinary, educational, and security services by service provider, on the part of urban households in 2004 EC.

Table 11.1: Frequency of respondents (household members) who accessed health services by provider

			Government		Private		Missions		NGOs		Total	
Woreda	**Town**	**All HHs**	**No. of HHs**	**%**	**No. of HHs**	**%**	**No. of HHs**	**%**	**No. Of HHs**	**%**	**No. Of HHs**	**%**
Dembiya	Qoladiba	50	48	96.0	6	12.0	3	6.0	0	0.0	49	98.0
Fogera	Woreta	50	20	40.0	27	54.0	3	6.0	0	0.0	34	68.0
Bahr Dar	Bahr Dar	100	52	52.0	40	40.0	4	4.0	2	2.0	73	73.0
Gondar Zuria	Maksegnit	50	46	92.0	13	26.0	0	0.0	0	0.0	47	94.0
Libo	Addis Zemen	50	34	68.0	15	30.0	0	0.0	0	0.0	40	80.0
Mecha	Merawi	50	38	76.0	28	56.0	1	2.0	0	0.0	41	82.0
Total (All sample towns)		350	238	68.0	129	36.9	11	3.1	2	0.6	284	81.1

SOURCE: Field Data

The study has established that an average of 238 hhs (68%) in the six urban centers accessed health services from government facilities, which is followed by 129 (37%) that were provided health care through private operators (table 11.1). The number of those who were provided health care by missionary societies and NGOs is 11 (3.1%) and 2 (0.6%) respectively. All in all, 284 households (81.1%) received health care from various sources during the year in question. The percentage of HHs that received health care in 2004 EC ranges from a minimum of 68% in Woreta (Fogera) to a maximum of 98% in Qoladiba (Dembiya) Towns.

The situation pertaining to access to veterinary services on the part of respondents from the six urban centers under study is low (Table 11.2). It was learnt that during the year under consideration, only 37 HHs (less than 11%) of the total reported that they received veterinary services. Of these, a majority of 25 (7.1%) accessed the services provided by the government followed by 17 (4.9%) that got the services from private providers. The number of those that used facilities of missionary societies and NGOs for accessing veterinary services is 1 (0.3%) and 0 (0%) respectively. The low rate of accessing veterinary services from various sources could be explained by the fact that the overwhelming majority of urban dwellers may not have livestock and this may have not prompted them to seek animal health services.

Table 11.2: Frequency of respondents (households members) who accessed veterinary services by providers

			Government		**Private**		**Mission**		**NGOs**		**Total**	
Woreda	**Town**	**All HHs**	**No. Of HHs**	**%**	**No. of HHs**	**%**	**No. Of HHs**	**%**	**No. Of HHs**	**%**	**No. Of HHs**	**%**
Dembiya	Qoladiba	50	7	14.0	1	2.0	0	0.0	0	0.0	7	14.0
Fogera	Woreta	50	8	16.0	6	12.0	0	0.0	0	0.0	14	28.0
Bahr Dar	Bahr Dar	100	0	0.0	2	2.0	0	0.0	0	0.0	2	2.0
Gondar Zuria	Maksegnit	50	2	4.0	0	0.0	1	2.0	0	0.0	3	6.0
Libo	Addis Zemen	50	2	4.0	0	0.0	0	0.0	0	0.0	2	4.0
Mecha	Merawi	50	6	12.0	8	16.0	0	0.0	0	0.0	9	18.0
Total (All sample towns)		350	25	7.1	17	4.9	1	0.3	0	0.0	37	10.6

SOURCE: Field Data

In regard to access to educational services, the percentage of affirmative responses in the study locations is provided in Table 11.3. The average percentage of respondents who claimed to have had access to educational services is 66% (231 HHs) of which a maximum of 82% and a minimum of 58% is recorded in Qoladiba (Dembiya) and Maksegnit (Gondar Zuria) respectively.

Table 11.3: Frequency of respondents (households members) who accessed educational services in 2004 EC

Woreda	Town	All HHs	No. of HHs	%
Dembiya	Qoladiba	50	41	82.0
Fogera	Woreta	50	34	68.0
Bahr Dar	Bahr Dar	100	63	63.0
Gondar Zuria	Maksegnit	50	29	58.0
Libo	Addis Zemen	50	30	60.0
Mecha	Merawi	50	34	68.0
Total (All sample towns)		350	231	66.0

SOURCE: Field Data

Concerning access to security services, the average percentage in all the urban centers under study is around 65% of which a minimum of 18% and a maximum of 92% are recorded in Woreta (Fogera) and Merawi (Mecha) respectively. Government sources are mentioned as the highest providers of security services by 223 respondents (63.7%). Among those who reported enjoying access to security services from the government, a minimum of 16% and a maximum of 90% were from Woreta (Fogera) and Merawi (Mecha). No respondent claimed to have obtained security services from other sources like private providers, missionary societies and NGOs (Table 11.4).

Table 11.4: Frequency and percentage of respondents (households members) with access to security services

			Government		Private		Missions		NGOs		Total	
Woreda	**Town**	**All HHs**	**No. of HHs**	**%**	**No. Of HHs**	**%**	**No. of HHs**	**%**	**No. of HHs**	**%**	**No. of HHs**	**%**
Dembiya	Qoladiba	50	43	86.0	0	0.0	0	0.0	0	0.0	43	86.0
Fogera	Woreta	50	8	16.0	0	0.0	1	2.0	0	0.0	9	18.0
Bahirdar	Bahr Dar	100	75	75.0	6	6.0	0	0.0	0	0.0	77	77.0
Gondar Zuria	Maksegnit	50	29	58.0	0	0.0	0	0.0	0	0.0	29	58.0
Libo	Addis Zemen	50	23	46.0	0	0.0	0	0.0	0	0.0	23	46.0
Mecha	Merawi	50	45	90.0	1	2.0	0	0.0	0	0.0	46	92.0
Total (All sample towns)		350	223	63.7	7	2.0	1	0.3	0	0.0	227	64.9

SOURCE: Field Data

11.2. State of School Enrollment

The study has endeavored to establish the frequency and percentage of respondents who reported the state of favorability of enrolling children to primary schools by designating the situation as very easy, easy, not easy, difficult, and very difficult. As indicated in Table 11.5, a combined frequency of 243 respondents (69.7%) stated that enrolling children in primary schools is very easy and easy whereas the number of those that found the situation between the range of not easy and very difficult is 44 (12.5%). As indicated in the Table, the highest percentage of respondents affirming that the situation is very easy was recorded in Qoladiba (58%) while 7% among those from Bahr Dar said that enrolling children in primary schools is very difficult. Among those who found the situation easy, the majority of 60% were from Addis Zemen (Libo).

Table 11.5: Frequency of respondents who reported state of enrolling children in primary schools

			Very easy		Easy		Not easy		Difficult		Very difficult	
Woreda	**Town**	**All HHs**	**No. of HHs**	**%**	**No. of HHs**	**%**	**No. Of HHs**	**%**	**No. Of HHs**	**%**	**No. Of HHs**	**%**
Dembiya	Qoladiba	50	29	58.0	22	44.0	0	0.0	0	0.0	1	2.0
Fogera	Woreta	50	14	28.0	24	48.0	2	4.0	3	6.0	0	0.0
Bahr Dar	Bahr Dar	100	6	6.0	35	35.0	13	13.0	13	13.0	7	7.0
Gondar Zuria	Maksegnit	50	20	40.0	18	36.0	0	0.0	0	0.0	0	0.0
Libo	Addis Zemen	50	15	30.0	30	60.0	1	2.0	0	0.0	0	0.0
Mecha	Merawi	50	16	32.0	14	28.0	2	4.0	2	4.0	0	0.0
Total (All sample towns)		350	100	28.6	143	40.9	18	5.1	18	5.1	8	2.3

SOURCE: Field Data

Regarding the state of enrolling children in secondary schools, the responses obtained from informants in the urban centers under study is provided in Table 11.6. Accordingly, the maximum number of those who reported that getting admission for their children in secondary schools as being easy is 33 (66%) in Addis Zemen (Libo). The total frequency and percentage of those who fall under this category in all the urban centers under study is 120 (34.3%). The combined frequency of informants who think enrolling children in secondary schools as not easy and very difficult is 59 (16.9%).

Table 11.6: Frequency of respondents who reported enrolling children in secondary schools has been easy or difficult

			Very easy		Easy		Not easy		Difficult		Very difficult	
Woreda	**Town**	**All HHs**	**No. Of HHs**	**%**	**No. of HHs**	**%**	**No. of HHs**	**%**	**No. of HHs**	**%**	**No. of HHs**	**%**
Dembiya	Qoladiba	50	26	52.0	20	40.0	0	0.0	0	0.0	0	0.0
Fogera	Woreta	50	5	10.0	21	42.0	2	4.0	3	6.0	1	2.0
Bahirdar	Bahr Dar	100	3	3.0	12	12.0	21	21.0	15	15.0	13	13.0
Gondar Zuria	Maksegnit	50	3	6.0	28	56.0	0	0.0	1	2.0	0	0.0
Libo	Addis Zemen	50	2	4.0	33	66.0	0	0.0	0	0.0	0	0.0
Mecha	Merawi	50	12	24.0	6	12.0	0	0.0	2	4.0	1	2.0
Total (All sample towns)		350	51	14.6	120	34.3	23	6.6	21	6.0	15	4.3

SOURCE: Field Data

11.3. Denial of access to primary education due to inability to pay

The percentage of respondents whose children were denied the opportunity of attending primary education due to their inability to pay is provided in Table 11.7. As indicated in the table, the number of those who reported that they have been denied access due to inability to pay is negligible ranging between a minimum of 0 in Addis Zemen (Libo) and a maximum of 4 each in Bahr Dar, Maksegnit and Merawi. A minimum of 2% and a maximum of 24% of the respondents in Qoladiba (Dembiya) and Woreta (Fogera) respectively stated that this is not applicable to them for various reasons like having no school-age children or other causes. All in all, a total of 77% of the respondents reported that they did not face hurdles in enrolling children in primary schools due to inability to pay. An average of 15.7% of respondents in the urban centers under study reported the query is not applicable to them.

Table 11.7: Percentage of respondents whose children were denied attending primary school due to inability to pay

			No		Yes		Not Applicable		Total	
Woreda	**Town**	**All HHs**	**No. of HHs**	**%**	**No. Of HHs**	**%**	**No. Of HHs**	**%**	**No. of HHs**	**%**
Dembiya	Qoladiba	50	47	94.0	1	2.0	1	2.0	49	98.0
Fogera	Woreta	50	31	62.0	2	4.0	12	24.0	45	90.0
Bahirdar	Bahr Dar	100	70	70.0	4	4.0	23	23.0	97	97.0
Gondar Zuria	Maksegnit	50	39	78.0	4	8.0	6	12.0	49	98.0
Libo	Addis Zemen	50	43	86.0	0	0.0	7	14.0	50	100.0
Mecha	Merawi	50	40	80.0	4	8.0	6	12.0	50	100.0
Total (All sample towns)		350	270	77.1	15	4.3	55	15.7	340	97.1

SOURCE: Field Data

11.4. Accessing medical services in terms of conduciveness

The frequency and percentage of respondents who reported the state of accessing medical services in terms of being very easy, easy, not easy, difficult, and very difficult in government facilities is illustrated in Table 11.8. Accordingly, an average percentage of 27.1% of the respondents in all study sites attested that the state of conduciveness in accessing medical services is very easy whereas those who reported the situation as easy is nearly 60%. The cumulative average percentage of those who described the situation as difficult and very difficult is 10.6%. Of those who reported very easy access, 36% were from Maksegnit (Gondar Zuria) followed by 18%, 17%, 13% and 12 % in Addis Zemen (Libo), Qoladiba (Dembiya), Woreta (Fogera) and Merawi (Mecha) respectively.

Table 11.8: Frequency of respondents who reported state of accessing government medical services

			Very easy		Easy		Not easy		Difficult		Very difficult	
Woreda	**Town**	**All HHs**	**No. of HHs**	**%**	**No. Of HHs**	**%**	**No. of HHs**	**%**	**No. Of HHs**	**%**	**No. of HHs**	**%**
Dembiya	Qoladiba	50	17	34.0	32	64.0	3	6.0	4	8.0	2	4.0
Fogera	Woreta	50	12	24.0	24	48.0	6	12.0	3	6.0	2	4.0
Bahr Dar	Bahr Dar	100	15	15.0	38	38.0	25	25.0	13	13.0	8	8.0
Gondar Zuria	Maksegnit	50	21	42.0	26	52.0	1	2.0	0	0.0	0	0.0
Libo	Addis Zemen	50	18	36.0	31	62.0	1	2.0	0	0.0	0	0.0
Mecha	Merawi	50	12	24.0	27	54.0	2	4.0	1	2.0	4	8.0
Total (All sample towns)		350	95	27.1	178	50.9	38	10.9	21	6.0	16	**4.6**

SOURCE: Field Data

State of affairs pertaining to the state of accessing medical services from private providers is illustrated in Table 11.9. In all the urban centers under study, the average combined percentage of those who described the situation as very easy and easy is 46.3% whereas a total of 32.6% stated that accessing medical services from private sources is not easy and difficult. There was no single respondent in all the study sites who stated access to private medical services as very difficult.

Table 11.9: Frequency of respondents who reported state of accessing private medical services

			Very easy		Easy		Not easy		Difficult		Very difficult	
Woreda	**Town**	**All HHs**	**No. Of HHs**	**%**	**No. Of HHs**	**%**	**No. of HHs**	**%**	**No. Of HHs**	**%**	**No. Of HHs**	**%**
Dembiya	Qoladiba	50	7	14.0	27	54.0	11	22.0	1	2.0	0	0.0
Fogera	Woreta	50	7	14.0	17	34.0	8	16.0	12	24.0	0	0.0
Bahr Dar	Bahr Dar	100	2	2.0	3	3.0	21	21.0	26	26.0	0	0.0
Gondar Zuria	Maksegnit	50	3	6.0	29	58.0	0	0.0	13	26.0	0	0.0
Libo	Addis	50	5	10.0	23	46.0	8	16.0	13	26.0	0	0.0

	Zemen											
Mecha	Merawi	50	26	52.0	13	26.0	1	2.0	0	0.0	0	0.0
Total (All sample towns)		350	50	14.3	112	32.0	49	14.0	65	18.6	0	0.0

SOURCE: Field Data

11.5. Denial of health services due to inability to pay

In the same vein, informants comprising the sample population were asked whether they have been denied of access to medical services due to their inability to pay (Table 11.10). Whereas a total average of 41.4% of the respondents in all the study sites reported that they were not denied access, 39.4% stated that they could not get health services due to inability to pay. On the other hand, an average of 4.6% of the respondents said that this query is not applicable to them probably due to the fact that they have either not sought the services or other causes.

Table 11.10: Frequency of respondents who were denied of accessing medical services due to inability to pay

			No		Yes		Not Applicable	
Woreda	**Town**	**All HHs**	**No. of HHs**	**%**	**No. of HHs**	**%**	**No. of HHs**	**%**
Dembiya	Qoladiba	50	37	74.0	5	10.0	0	0.0
Fogera	Woreta	50	14	28.0	18	36.0	3	6.0
Bahr Dar	Bahr Dar	100	71	71.0	6	6.0	12	12.0
Gondar Zuria	Maksegnit	50	13	26.0	29	58.0	0	0.0
Libo	Addis Zemen	50	10	20.0	31	62.0	0	0.0
Mecha	Merawi	50	0	0.0	49	98.0	1	2.0
Total (All sample towns)		350	145	41.4	138	39.4	16	4.6

SOURCE: Field Data

11.6. Access to services and distance covered

Another issue that the study raised pertains to the average time that the respondents travel in order to access services like grain mills, and primary and secondary schools and the number of households that have access to these services (Table 11.11). Accordingly, it was learnt that 99% of the respondents claimed access to the services. It was also reported that the average time taken to reach secondary schools in all the urban centers under study is 23.2 minutes ranging between a minimum of 14.5 minutes and a maximum of 30.8 minutes by those from Woreta (Fogera) and Merawi (Mecha) respectively. Individually taken, the average time traveled to access grain mills and primary schools in all the study sites is reported as 10.4 and 16.8 minutes respectively. In the first case (grain mill centers), the average distance covered is within a minimum range of 6.2 minutes in Addis Zemen (Libo) and 18.9 minutes in Bahr Dar whereas in the latter (primary schools), the range is between a minimum of 13.6 minutes in Qoladiba (Dembiya) and 22.1 minutes in Woreta (Fogera).

Table 11.11: Frequency of respondents having access to grain mills, and primary and secondary schools

			Grain mill			Primary school			Secondary school		
Woreda	**Town**	**All HHs**	**% HHs**	**Average Time (minutes)**	**Min-max Time (minutes)**	**% HHs**	**Average time (minutes)**	**Min-max time (minutes**	**% HHs**	**Average Time (minutes)**	**Min-max time (minutes**
Dembiya	Qoladiba	50	98	8.4	1-30	98	13.6	5-40	98	15.3	5-40
Fogera	Woreta	50	96	10.7	3-40	98	22.1	10-60	98	14.5	5-30
Bahr Dar	Bahr Dar	100	98	18.9	1-50	98	18.9	5-50	98	31.2	0-60
Godar Zuria	Maksegnit	50	100	6.6	0-30	100	16.9	5-60	100	23.3	10-40
Libo	Addis Zemen	50	100	6.2	2-20	100	14.1	4-30	98	23.9	2-50
Mecha	Merawi	50	100	11.7	3-51	100	15.4	1-30	100	30.8	0-45
Total (All sample towns)		**350**	**99**	**10.4**	**0 – 50**	**99**	**16.8**	**1 - 60**	**99**	**23.2**	**0 – 60**

SOURCE: Field Data

A similar query was also posed in regard to the percentage of households that have access to health posts, health centers and veterinary service centers and the time taken to reach them (Table 11.12). As indicated by the figures in the table, 40%, 39% and 93% of all households in the study sites have access to health posts, health centers, and veterinary services respectively. The average time traveled to access the aforementioned services is 9.1, 16.7 and 16.5 minutes respectively. The percentage of respondent HHS who has access to health posts lies between a minimum of 4% (in Woreta, Maksegnit and Addis Zemen) and a maximum of 96% in Qoladiba (Dembiya). In regard to access to health posts, the average percentage range is between 0% in Qoladiba, Woreta and Bahr Dar and a maximum of 100% in Addis Zemen (Libo). On the other hand, the percentage of HHs that has access to veterinary services is considerably high ranging between a minimum of 77% (Bahr Dar) and a maximum of 100% (in Maksegnit, Addis Zemen and Merawi).

Table 11.12: Frequency of respondents having access to health posts, health centers and veterinary services

			Health post			Health center			Veterinary service		
Woreda	**Town**	**All HHs**	**% HHs**	**Average time (minutes)**	**Min-max Time (minutes**	**% HHs**	**Average time (minutes)**	**Min-max time (minutes**	**% of HHs**	**Average Time (minutes)**	**Min-max Time (minutes**
Dembiya	Qoladiba	50	96	24.8	5-40	0	-	-	96	17.2	10-30
Fogera	Woreta	50	4	15.0	0-30	0	-	-	98	30.4	10-60
Bahr Dar	Bahr Dar	100	83	1.1	0-60	0	-	-	77	2.7	0-50
Gondar Zuria	Maksegnit	50	4	0.0	0-0	98	16.1	5-40	100	17.0	0-40
Libo	Addis Zemen	50	4	10.0	10-10	100	13.9	5-30	100	21.1	2-40
Mecha	Merawi	50	6	4.0	0-12	78	20.1	10-51	100	10.8	1-40
Total (All sample towns)		350	40	9.1	0 - 60	39	16.7	5 - 51	93	16.5	0 – 60

SOURCE: Field Data

Table 11.13 deals with issues concerning access and average travel time to water points, post offices and police stations. Accordingly, it was reported that 95%, 98% and 99% of the respondent HHs have access to these services respectively. The average time taken to reach the service centers is 8.3 minutes to water points, 18.7 minutes to post offices and 16.9 minutes to police stations by respondents in all the study sites. In terms of access to water points, the average percentage ranges from a minimum of 78% of HHs in Merawi (Mecha) to a maximum of 100% in Maksegnit (Gondar Zuria) and Addis Zemen (Libo). As regards access to post offices, a minimum of 96% in Qoladiba (Dembiya) and a maximum of 100% of HHs in Maksegnit, Addis Zemen and Merawi are recorded.

Table 11.13: Frequency of respondents having access to water points, post offices, and police stations

		Water point				Post office			Police Station		
Woreda	**Town**	**All HHs**	**% HHs**	**Average time (minutes)**	**Min-max time (minutes**	**% HHs**	**Average time (minutes)**	**Min-max time (minutes**	**% HHs**	**Average time (minutes)**	**Min-max time (minutes**
Dembiya	Qoladiba	50	98	4.0	0-25	96	14.2	5-25	98	17.5	3-50
Fogera	Woreta	50	98	16.4	1-60	98	13.7	0-60	98	18.9	5-40
Bahr Dar	Bahr Dar	100	97	3.2	0-60	97	29.1	0-70	97	16.2	1-50
Gondar Zuria	Maksegnit	50	100	19.3	0-90	100	12.7	5-40	100	11.0	2-30
Libo	Addis Zemen	50	100	5.0	1-60	100	16.4	5-30	100	13.3	3-30
Mecha	Merawi	50	78	1.6	0-22	100	25.8	8-60	100	24.5	5-40
Total (All sample towns)		350	95	8.3	0 – 90	98	18.7	0 - 80	99	16.9	1 - 50

SOURCE: Field Data

The percentage of respondents with access to market centers and telecommunication services including the time taken to reach these services is provided in Table 11.14. As shown in the table, 99% and 88% of the respondent HHs have access to market centers and telecommunications services in the study sites. The percentage of HHs with access to market centers is within a range of a minimum of 97% in Bahr Dar and a maximum of 100% in Maksegnit, Addis Zemen and Merawi whereas a minimum of 40% in Maksegnit and a maximum of 98% each in Qoladiba and Woreta are reported to have access telecommunication services. The travel time taken to market centers is stated as a minimum of 9.5 minutes in Maksegnit (Gondar Zuria) and a maximum of 27.6 minutes in Bahr Dar while a minimum of 9.8 minutes and a maximum of 26 minutes to reach telecommunication centers is recorded in Addis Zemen (Libo) and Merawi (Mecha) respectively.

Table 11.14: Frequency of respondents having access to market centers and telecommunication services

			Market center				Telecommunication		
Woreda	**Town**	**All HHs**	**% of HHs**	**Average time (minutes)**	**Min-max time (minutes**	**% of HHs**	**Average Time (minutes)**	**Min-max time (minutes**
Dembiya	Qoladiba	50	98	12.8	5-50	98	12.4	1-30
Fogera	Woreta	50	98	18.4	5-40	98	19.3	10-40
Bahr Dar	Bahr Dar	100	97	27.6	0-60	96	25.9	0-60
Gondar Zuria	Maksegnit	50	100	9.5	2-30	40	12.1	1-30
Libo	Addis Zemen	50	100	11.9	5-30	92	9.8	0-30
Mecha	Merawi	50	100	12.8	2-30	96	26.0	8-60
Total (All sample towns)		350	99	10.4	0 - 60	88	17.6	0 - 80

SOURCE: Field Data

XII. ASSETS

In this section, the findings of the study regarding the possession of assets of respondent households are described. As is clear, one of the major objectives of this baseline study is to show whether households in the study areas have registered periodic improvements in terms of creating and accumulating assets as a result of betterments induced by development projects in the sub-basin. It is hoped that the baseline study will serve as a point of reference to determine changes and continuities with regard to the state of livelihoods of communities inhabiting the different geographic locations covered as the study sites.

12.1. Possession of various assets

Attempt is made to record the possession of assets in the form of livestock, residential units, production tools and instruments, furniture and other household utilities, financial savings including their values where applicable. The figures in Table 12.1 describe the percentage of household heads who reported ownership of livestock and residential units along with their monetary value. As indicated, an average of 65% and 20% of the respondents in the urban centers under study respectively stated that they own livestock and residential units that have average worth of Birr 50,000 and Birr 8950 respectively. The percentage of respondents who reported that they possess livestock is between a minimum of 32% in Qoladiba (Dembiya) and a maximum of 96% in Addis Zemen (Libo). Whereas a minimum average price of 30000 Birr for livestock owned by 96% of the respondents in Addis Zemen (Libo) is recorded, the average price of livestock possessed by 64 respondents in Merawi (Mecha) is registered as Birr 70,000. As shown in the table, the average percentage of people owning residential units in the study sites is only 20% with an average worth ranging from a minimum of Birr 1600 in Maksegnit (Gondar Zuria) to a maximum of 12500 Birr in Bahr Dar and Merawi (Mecha) each.

Table 12.1: Percentage of respondents possessing the indicated assets and average price of the assets

			Livestock		House	
Woreda	**Town**	**All HHs**	**% of HHs having the asset**	**Current price (median)**	**% of HHs having the asset**	**current price (median)**
Dembiya	Qoladiba	50	32	50000	16	1750
Fogera	Woreta	50	94	40000	56	10500
Bahr Dar	Bahr Dar	100	48	60000	20	12500
Gondar Zuria	Maksegnit	50	76	50000	12	1600
Libo	Addis Zemen	50	96	30000	20	7400
Mecha	Merawi	50	64	70000	16	12500
Total (All sample towns)		350	65	50000	20	8950

SOURCE: Field Data

Table 12.2 contains data on the possession of production tools like sewing machine and handicraft loom including their current monetary value. It was learnt that only 1% of the respondents reported that that they own sewing machines whose average monetary value is Birr 3750. Of these, no respondent claimed possessing sewing machine in Woreta (Fogera), Addis Zemen (Libo) and Merawi (Mecha). On the other hand, 4% and 2% each from among the respondents in Qoladiba (Dembiya) and Bahr Dar and Maksegnit (Gondar Zuria) respectively stated that they own sewing machines. Regarding ownership of handicraft loom, the percentage of respondents who claimed to own this implement is 3% with an average value of Birr 850.

Table 12.2: Percentage of respondents possessing sewing machine, handicraft loom, and other assets by average price

			Sewing machine			Handicraft loom			Others		
Woreda	**Town**	**All HHs**	**% of HHs Having the asset**	**current price (median)**	**Min-max Current price**	**% of HHs Having the asset**	**current price (median)**	**Min-max current price**	**% of HHs having The asset**	**current price (median)**	**Min-max current price**
Dembiya	Qoladiba	50	4	3750	2500 - 5000	10	350	200 - 400	-	-	-
Fogera	Woreta	50	0		-	0		-	-	-	-
Bahr Dar	Bahr Dar	100	2	5500	5000 - 6000	2	5250	500 - 10000	-	-	-
Gondar Zuria	Maksegnit	50	2	2000	2000 - 2000	0		-	-	-	-
Libo	Addis Zemen	50	0		-	4	850	200 - 1500	-	-	-
Mecha	Merawi	50	0		-	0		-	-	-	-
Total (All sample towns)		350	1	3750	-	3	850	-	-	-	-

SOURCE: Field Data

By the same token, queries on ownership of household items like TV sets, radio and tape recorders generated data that is contained in Table 12.3. Accordingly, 50%, 22% and 30% of the respondents were reported as owning TV sets, radios and tape recorders respectively in all the study locations. The median price of TV sets, radios and tape recorders owned by respondents in all the urban centers under study is recorded as Birr 3050, Birr 250 and Birr 425 respectively. In terms of percentage of respondents owning each of these household items, maximum possession of TV sets is recorded by 75% in Bahr Dar while Qoladiba (Dembiya) fared the least by registering ownership by 28% of the households. In regard to possession of radio sets, a maximum of 30% and a minimum of 12 % of respondents in Merawi (Mecha) and Maksegnit (Gondar Zuria) respectively were reported as owning radio sets. A maximum of 47% in Bahr Dar and a minimum of 10% in Maksegnit (Gondar Zuria) respectively claimed to own tape recorders.

Ownership of household items like refrigerators, jewelry, beds and chairs by percentage of households and monetary value is provided in Table 12.4.

12.2. Location of savings

Information on locations like banks, savings and credit unions, own residential units, and with relatives where financial savings of respondents are kept is illustrated in Table 12.7. As shown in the table, 76 respondents (21.7%) stated that their savings are deposited in banks whereas 17 (4.9%) have their savings kept in savings and credit unions. Nine respondents (2.6%) reported that they keep their savings at home. Only 2 (0.6%) respondents from Bahr Dar mentioned that they entrusted relatives to keep their savings. The percentage of those who deposited their savings in banks ranges from a minimum of 6% in Qoladiba (Dembiya) and Maksegnit (Gondar Zuria) to a maximum of 35% in Bahr Dar.

12.3. Membership in revolving fund schemes (iqub) and amount of weekly/monthly contribution

The results of the query on whether respondents are members of revolving fund schemes (iqub) and the amount of weekly/monthly contributions that they make is provided in Table 12.8. In all the study locations, an average of only 18 (5.1%) participate in the scheme. In this regard, the percentage of those who are members is reported as ranging between a minimum of 0% in Addis Zemen (Libo) and a maximum of 36% in Merawi (Mecha). The median and mean weekly/monthly contribution made by those who are members of such schemes in all the urban centers under study is Birr 75 and Birr 205 respectively.

12.4. Borrowing and outstanding debt

Data resulting from inquiries whether respondents have borrowed money from various sources during the first quarter of 2004 EC is illustrated in Table 12.9. It was learnt that during the period in question, a total of 21 respondents (6%) have borrowed money of which 8 (2.3%) borrowed from various organizations and the sources of 11 (3.1%) were individual lenders. Only 1 individual from Merawi (Mecha) stated that the sources were both organizations and individuals.

Regarding the query whether borrowers still carry outstanding debts, a total of 11 (3.1%) responded in the affirmative and reported that the median and mean of outstanding debts still holding are Birr 2500 and Birr 2851 respectively (Table 12.10).

12.5. Level of Education

Table 12.11 contains information on the level of education of respondents ranging from illiteracy to pursuit of formal education up to diploma level as part of human capital. As shown in the table, the level of formal education attained by respondents in all the study locations is diverse. Accordingly, 88 (25.1%) can neither read nor write, 15 (4.3%) can only read and write, and 53 (15.1%) and 40 (11.4%) have primary and junior secondary level education respectively. Those numbers and percentage of those who have secondary and diploma and above-level education are 46 (13.1%) and 34 (9.7%) respectively.

12.6. Skills

Data regarding the skills that the respondents command in various fields is illustrated in Table 12.12. An average of a significant majority of 64% in all the study locations pleaded that they do not possess skills that are worthy of mention Theses range from a minimum of 18% in Bahr Dar and 98% in Qoladiba (Dembiya). The percentage of respondents among the urban dwellers that reported having other skills including farming is 10.3% among which a maximum of 30% is reported by those in Bahr Dar. The average percentage of responses by those who claimed as having skills in carpentry, masonry, plumbing, mechanical knowledge, tailoring and management is recorded as 4.3%, 2.3%, 0.6%, 3.4%, 1.4%, and 3.1% respectively.

12.7. Support from relatives

Information was elicited whether respondents who are urban dwellers receive various types of support from relatives in the rural areas (Table 12.13). In all the study locations, a total of 121 (34.6%) stated that they receive support of various sorts from their relatives living in the rural areas. The percentage of those who responded in the affirmative to this query ranges from a minimum of 1% in Bahr Dar to a maximum of 88% in Addis Zemen (Libo), which is followed by 76% in Maksegnit (Gondar Zuria), 74% in Merawi (Mecha), 2% in Qoladiba (Dembiya), 1% in Bahr Dar, and 0% in Woreta (Fogera).

12.8 Neighborhood associations and mutual support

Of the total of 350 respondents in the urban areas under study, only 32% reported that they are members of neighborhood associations through which they get various types of support (table 12.14). The percentage of those who are members of such associations ranges from a bare minimum of 0% in Woreta (Fogera) to a maximum of 98% in Addis Zemen (Libo), followed by 70% in Maksegnit (Gondar Zuria), 52% in Merawi (Mecha), 2% in Qoladiba (Dembiya), and 1% in Bahr Dar.

Table 12.3: Percentage of respondents possessing TV, radio, tape recorder by average price

			TV set			Radio			Tape recorder			Telephone		
Woreda	**Town**	**All HHs**	**% of HHs having the asset**	**current price (median)**	**Min-max current price**	**% of HHs having the asset**	**current price (median)**	**Min-max time (minutes**	**% of HHs having the asset**	**current price (median)**	**Min-max time (minutes**	**% of HHs having the asset**	**current price (median)**	**Min-max time (minutes**
Dembiya	Qoladiba	50	28	2700	34 – 3000	24	200	100 - 400	32	375	150 - 5000	54	500	300 – 2150
Fogera	Woreta	50	36	4000	2500 – 7000	28	300	40 - 3300	16	450	250 - 2000	8	275	100 – 700
Bahr Dar Gondar Zuria	Bahr Dar	100	75	3000	900 – 90000	22	525	80 – 25000	47	1800	240 - 30000	40	314	210 – 12000
	Maksegnit	50	40	3000	2000 – 7000	12	125	50 - 350	10	500	350 - 900	12	335	200 – 500
Libo	Addis Zemen	50	38	3100	1 – 5600	16	200	1 – 500	18	400	140 - 1600	2	300	300 – 300
Mecha	Merawi	50	58	3250	350 – 7000	30	300	100 – 1100	40	250	80 - 1200	32	310	310 – 4000
Total (All sample towns)		350	50	3050	-	22	250	-	30	425	-	27	312	-

SOURCE: Field Data

Table 12.4: Percentage of respondents possessing refrigerator, jewelry, bed and chair by average price

			Refrigerator		Jewelry	Bed			Chair					
Woreda	**Town**	**All HHs**	**% HHs**	**Current price (median)**	**Min-max current price**	**% HHs**	**Current price (median)**	**Min-max current price**	**% HHs**	**current price (median)**	**Min-max time (minutes**	**% of HHs having the asset**	**Current price (median)**	Min-max time (minutes
Dembiya	Qoladiba	50	10	3000	2000 - 4000	22	1050	200 - 3000	92	625	100 - 4700	20	400.0	100 – 3000
Fogera	Woreta	50	6	6500	300 - 7000	26	2000	600 - 25000	96	1500	100 - 33000	24	200.0	20 – 4500
Bahr Dar	Bahr Dar	100	49	9000	1000 - 15000	49	5000	300 - 30000	86	3000	200 - 300000	70	500.0	1 – 6000
Gondar Zuria	Maksegnit	50	8	7000	7000 - 9000	14	6000	1800 - 15000	80	600	50 - 5000	22	35.0	10 – 1000
Libo	Addis Zemen	50	10	4500	4000 - 6200	22	2000	150 - 5000	86	700	50 - 6500	26	100.0	5 – 6000
Mecha	Merawi	50	14	8000	500 - 9000	32	2500	600 - 10000	88	1500	50 - 5500	64	500.0	50 – 5000
Total (All sample towns)		350	21	6750	-	31	2250	-	88	1100	-	42	300.0	-

SOURCE: Field Data

Table 12.5: Percentage of respondents possessing tables, sofa, and electric stove

				Tables		Sofa	Electric stove
Woreda	**Town**	**All HHs**	**% owners**	**current price (median)**	**% HHs**	**current price (median)**	**% HHs**
Dembiya	Qoladiba	50	22	200	4	5500	2
Fogera	Woreta	50	58	100	28	5000	0
Bahr Dar	Bahr Dar	100	75	300	44	7750	26
Gondar Zuria	Maksegnit	50	26	50	24	3050	0
Libo	Addis Zemen	50	48	100	14	3000	0
Mecha	Merawi	50	66	200	40	5500	2
Total (All sample towns)		350	53	150	28	5250	8

SOURCE: Field Data

Table 12.6: Percentage of respondents having any financial savings

			Yes		No	
Woreda	**Town**	**All HHs**	**No. of HHs**	**%**	**No. of HHs**	**%**
Dembiya	Qoladiba	50	15	30.0	35	70.0
Fogera	Woreta	50	11	22.0	39	78.0
Bahr Dar	Bahr Dar	100	47	47.0	53	53.0
Gondar Zuria	Maksegnit	50	5	10.0	45	90.0
Libo	Addis Zemen	50	9	18.0	41	82.0
Mecha	Merawi	50	21	42.0	29	58.0
Total (All sample towns)		350	108	30.9	242	69.1

SOURCE: Field Data

Table 12.7: Percentage of respondents having any financial savings by place of saving

				Banks	Saving credit unions			at home	With Relatives	
Woreda	**Town**	**AllHHs**	**No.HHs**	**%**	**No. of HHs**	**%**	**No.HHs**	**%**	**No. HHs**	**%**
Dembiya	Qoladiba	50	3	6.0	4	8.0	7	14.0	0	0.0
Fogera	Woreta	50	11	22.0	0	0.0	0	0.0	0	0.0
Bahr Dar	Bahr Dar	100	35	35.0	6	6.0	2	2.0	2	2.0
Gondar Zuria	Maksegnit	50	3	6.0	2	4.0	0	0.0	0	0.0
Libo	Addis Zemen	50	7	14.0	2	4.0	0	0.0	0	0.0
Mecha	Merawi	50	17	34.0	3	6.0	0	0.0	0	0.0
Total (All sample towns)		350	76	21.7	17	4.9	9	2.6	2	0.6

SOURCE: Field Data

le 12.8: Percentage of respondents who have membership in iqub by amount of contribution

			Members of iqub			
eda	**Town**	**All HHs**	**No. of HHs**	**%**	**Weekly/monthly contribution (median)**	**Weekly/monthly contribution Mean**
biya	Qoladiba	50	6	12.0	70	138
ra	Woreta	50	2	4.0	304	304
Dar	Bahr Dar	100	19	19.0	150	366
lar Zuria	Maksegnit	50	5	10.0	20	30
	Addis Zemen	50	0	0.0		
ıa	Merawi	50	18	36.0	75	186
(All sample towns)		350	18	5.1	75	205

JRCE: Field Data

		All HHs borrowed money			Borrowed from orgs		Borrowed from individuals		Borrowed from both	
eda	Town	All HHs	No. of HHs	%	No. of HHs	%	No. of HHs	%	No. of HHs	%
biya	Qoladiba	50	2	4.0	1	2.0	1	2.0	0	0.0
ra	Woreta	50	4	8.0	0	0.0	4	8.0	0	0.0
Dar	Bahr Dar	100	8	8.0	6	6.0	2	2.0	0	0.0
lar Zuria	Maksegnit	50	3	6.0	0	0.0	3	6.0	0	0.0
	Addis Zemen	50	1	2.0	0	0.0	0	0.0	0	0.0
ıa	Merawi	50	3	6.0	1	2.0	1	2.0	1	2.0
(All sample towns)		350	21	6.0	8	2.3	11	3.1	1	0.3

JRCE: Field Data

Table 12.10: Percentage of respondents who carry outstanding debt by amount of the debt

			All HHs carrying outstanding debt			
Woreda	**Town**	**All HHs**	**No. of HHs**	**%**	**Median**	**Mean**
Dembiya	Qoladiba	50	2	4.0	1600	1600
Fogera	Woreta	50	1	2.0	2000	2000
Bahr Dar	Bahr Dar	100	7	7.0	3000	3806
Gondar Zuria	Maksegnit	50	-	-	-	-
Libo	Addis Zemen	50	1	2.0	4000	4000
Mecha	Merawi	50	-	-	-	-
Total (All sample towns)		350	11	3.1	2500	2851

SOURCE: Field Data

Table 12.11: Percentage of respondents (household heads) by level of education

			None		Read & write only		Primary		Junior secondary		Secondary		Diploma Plus	
Woreda	Town	All HHs	No. HHs	%	No. HHs	%	No. HHs	%	No. HHs	%	No. HHs	%	No. HHs	%
Dembiya	Qoladiba	50	5	10.0	3	6.0	7	14.0	5	10.0	6	12.0	5	10.0
Fogera	Woreta	50	19	38.0	3	6.0	8	16.0	7	14.0	2	4.0	7	14.0
Bahr Dar	Bahr Dar	100	13	13.0	4	4.0	11	11.0	20	20.0	20	20.0	8	8.0
Gondar Zuria	Maksegnit	50	19	38.0	0	0.0	11	22.0	2	4.0	6	12.0	3	6.0
Libo	Addis Zemen	50	21	42.0	0	0.0	7	14.0	3	6.0	4	8.0	5	10.0
Mecha	Merawi	50	11	22.0	5	10.0	9	18.0	3	6.0	8	16.0	6	12.0
Total (All sample towns)		350	88	25.1	15	4.3	53	15.1	40	11.4	46	13.1	34	9.7

SOURCE: Field Data

			Carpentry	**Masonry**	**Plumbing**	**Mechanic**	**Tailoring**	**Managerial**	**Others including farming**	**No skill**
Woreda	**Town**	**All HHs**	**%**	**%**	**%**	**%**	**%**	**%**	**%**	**%**
Dembiya	Qoladiba	50	0.0	0.0	0.0	0.0	0.0	0.0	0.0	98.0
Fogera	Woreta	50	6.0	0.0	0.0	2.0	0.0	0.0	2.0	76.0
Bahr Dar	Bahr Dar	100	6.0	7.0	1.0	5.0	4.0	11.0	30.0	18.0
Gondar Zuria	Maksegnit	50	6.0	0.0	2.0	4.0	0.0	0.0	2.0	72.0
Libo	Addis Zemen	50	6.0	0.0	0.0	4.0	2.0	0.0	4.0	80.0
Mecha	Merawi	50	0.0	2.0	0.0	4.0	0.0	0.0	4.0	86.0
Total (All sample towns)		350.0	4.3	2.3	0.6	3.4	1.4	3.1	10.3	64.0

SOURCE: Field Data

Table 12.13: Percentage of respondents (HHs) who receive support from rural relatives

Woreda	Town	All HHs	No. of HHs	%
Dembiya	Qoladiba	50	1	2.0
Fogera	Woreta	50	0	0.0
Bahr Dar	Bahr Dar	100	1	1.0
Gondar Zuria	Maksegnit	50	38	76.0
Libo	Addis Zemen	50	44	88.0
Mecha	Merawi	50	37	74.0
Total (All sample towns)		350	121	34.6

SOURCE: Field Data

Table 12.14: Percentage of respondents (household heads) who are members of neighborhood associations by type of support

		% HHs having neighborhood association	
Woreda	Town	All HHs	%
Dembiya	Qoladiba	50	2.0
Fogera	Woreta	50	0.0
Bahr Dar	Bahr Dar	100	1.0
Gondar Zuria	Maksegnit	50	70.0
Libo	Addis Zemen	50	98.0
Mecha	Merawi	50	52.0
Total (All sample towns)		350.0	32.0

SOURCE: Field Data

XIII. HOUSING

13.1. House Ownership, Housing Conditions and Facilities

Under this section, informants were asked to provide data on status of ownership of houses, the conditions of residential units in which they dwell and the facilities that are available in the house. Table 13.1 illustrates the status of respondents' ownership of residential units by type in the urban centers and woredas under study. As indicated in the Table, 47% of the total respondents stated that they own non-storied detached residential units. The percentage of those in this category is the highest (98%) in Qoladiba, followed by 75%, 38%, 34%, 8% and 0% in Bahr Dar, Maksegnit, Addis Zemen, Woreta and Merawi respectively. The average percentage of those dwelling in non-storied attached houses is 33.7% of the total of which a maximum of 90% are in Woreta and a minimum of 0% are from Qoladiba and Merawi. On the other hand 100% of the respondents from Merawi reported that they live in mud houses followed by 28% in Maksegnit who were found to be in the same category.

Table 13.1: Percentage of respondents who own houses by type

			Type of House			
Woreda	**Town**	**All HHs**	**% Non-storied detached**	**% Non-storied attached**	**% Other (Mud house)**	**Total**
Dembiya	Qoladiba	50	98.0	0.0	0.0	98.0
Fogera	Woreta	50	8	90.0	0.0	98.0
Bahr Dar	Bahr Dar	100	75	23.0	0.0	98.0
Gander Zuria	Maksegnit	50	38	34.0	28.0	100.0
Libo	Addis Zemen	50	34	66.0	0.0	100.0
Mecha	Merawi	50	0	0.0	100.0	100.0
Total (All sample towns)		350	47	33.7	18.3	98.9

SOURCE: Field Data

Data regarding the floor area of residential units owned by respondents in the town under study is provided in Table 13.2. Of the total respondents interviewed in the urban centers under study, the percentage of those who reported the floor area of their houses as being between 25 sq meters and 49 sq meters is over 35.1%. Among these, majorities of 68% and 54% were from Woreta and Addis Zemen respectively. Of the average percentage of 26% the floor area of their houses are less than 25 sq meters, 50% and 40 % were from Maksegnit and Addis Zemen respectively. On the other hand, the average percentage of respondents with houses on greater than or equal to 75 sq meters is 16.3% of which 44% and 34% are from Merawi and Qoladiba respectively.

Table 13.2: Percentage of respondents who reported owned houses by floor area

			Floor Area (Sq. meter)		
Woreda	**Town**	**All HHs**	**% of HHs with < 25 sq. mts**	**% of HHs with 25-49 sq.mts**	**% of HHs with > =75 sq.mts**
Dembiya	Qoladiba	50	0.0	22.0	34.0
Fogera	Woreta	50	18	68.0	6.0
Bahr Dar	Bahr Dar	100	29	15.0	12.0
G/Zuria	Maksegnit	50	50	46.0	4.0
Libo	Addis Zemen	50	40	54.0	2.0
Mecha	Merawi	50	16	26.0	44.0
Total (All sample towns)		350	26	35.1	16.3

SOURCE: Field Data

Respondents were asked to specify the mode of acquisition and type of tenure under their residential units. Accordingly, it was learnt that 57% of the respondents interviewed in all urban centers under study own the houses in which they live (table 13.3). Of these the majority of 94% were in Woreta followed by 58% and 56% each in Addis Zemen, and Maksegnit and Merawi respectively. The highest percentages of 38% in Qoladiba live in houses rented from kebeles whereas 44% in Merawi live in houses rented from individuals. Only 4% of the informants in Qoladiba stated as living in houses for which they do not pay rent.

Table 13.3: Percentage of respondents who reported house owned by tenure type

			Tenure type				
Woreda	**Town**	**All HHs**	**% Owner occupied**	**% Rented from kebele**	**% Rented from private HHs**	**% Rent-free**	**% Others**
Dembiya	Qoladiba	50	26.0	38.0	28.0	4.0	2.0
Fogera	Woreta	50	94	0.0	6.0	0.0	0.0
Bahr Dar	Bahr Dar	100	53	21.0	25.0	0.0	1.0
G/Zuria	Maksegnit	50	56	2.0	42.0	0.0	0.0
Libo	Addis Zemen	50	58	26.0	16.0	0.0	0.0
Mecha	Merawi	50	56	0.0	44.0	0.0	0.0
Total (All sample towns)		350	57	15.4	26.6	0.6	0.6

SOURCE: Field Data

The percentage of respondents who reported house owned by mode of ownership (purchased/built by own money, purchased/built through bank loan, inherited, gift from relative/friend, aid donation, other) by town and study woreda is provided in Table 13.4. Of a total of 197 informants who reported that they own the houses in which they live, a majority of 78% possessed their residential units through purchasing or building by using own money.

Table 13.4: Percentage of respondents who reported the mode of ownership of houses in which they live

			Mode of ownership				
Woreda	**Town**	**All HHs who owned house**	**% Purchased /built with own money**	**% Purchased /built with bank money**	**% In herited**	**% Gift from relati ve/ friend**	**% Othe r**
Dembiya	Qoladiba	13	61.5	0.0	15.4	15.4	7.7
Fogera	Woreta	47	93.6	4.3	0.0	2.1	0.0
Bahr Dar	Bahr Dar	53	67.9	3.8	9.4	1.9	17.0
G/Zuria	Maksegnit	28	92.9	0.0	0.0	3.6	3.6
Libo	Addis Zemen	29	93.1	6.9	0.0	0.0	0.0

Mecha	Merawi	27	44.4	0.0	3.7	3.7	48.1
Total (All sample towns)		197	78	3.0	4.1	3.0	12.2

SOURCE: Field Data

The figures in Table 13.5 illustrate the amount of monthly rent that respondents pay for the residential units in which they live. Of the 146 informants who reported that they live in rented houses, an average of 32% pay monthly rents of less than 25 birr whereas 28% incur monthly expenses of about Birr 150 to cover their house rents. The average percentage of those who pay between Birr 25 and 75 for house rent is 15%.

Table 13.5: Percentage of respondents by amount of monthly rent they pay for the house in which they live

			Monthly rent (Birr/ month)			
Woreda	**Town**	**All HHs Rented a house**	**% < 25 birr/month**	**25 – 75 birr/month**	**75 - 150 birr/month**	**>= 150 birr month**
Dembiya	Qoladiba	33	57.6	18.2	21.2	3.0
Fogera	Woreta	3	0	0.0	33.3	66.7
Bahr Dar	Bahr Dar	45	35.6	17.8	13.3	33.3
G/Zuria	Maksegnit	22	4.55	18.2	40.9	36.4
Libo	Addis Zemen	21	52.4	14.3	28.6	4.8
Mecha	Merawi	22	0	4.5	31.8	63.6
Total (All sample towns)		146	32	15.1	24.7	28.1

SOURCE: Field Data

The percentage of respondents who reported the number of rooms in their houses is provided in Table 13.6. Of the total of 350 respondents in all the urban centers under study, an average percentage of 50% lives in residential units having between 1 and 2 rooms. Of these, the great majority of 82% are in Qoladiba, followed by 78% and 62% in Addis Zemen and Maksegnit respectively. The average percentage of those living in houses with 3-4 rooms is 39.7% of which 72% are from Woreta.

Table 13.6: Percentage of respondents by number of rooms in their residential units

			Number of rooms per household							
Woreda	**Town**	**All HHs**	**% of HHs with 1 - 2 rooms**	**% of HHs with 3 - 4 rooms**	**% of HHs with 5 – 6 rooms**	**% of HHs with >= 7 rooms**	**Mean**	**Median**	**Min**	**Max**
Dembiya	Qoladiba	50	82.0	16.0	0.0	0.0	1.6	1.0	1.0	4.0
Fogera	Woreta	50	28	72.0	0.0	0.0	2.8	3.0	1.0	4.0
Bahr Dar G/Zuria	Bahr Dar	100	38	29.0	14.0	12.0	4.0	3.0	1.0	23.0
	Maksegnit	50	62	38.0	0.0	0.0	2.2	2.0	1.0	3.0
Libo	Addis Zemen	50	78	22.0	0.0	0.0	2.0	2.0	1.0	3.0
Mecha	Merawi	50	24	72.0	4.0	0.0	2.9	3.0	1.0	5.0
Total (All sample towns)		350	50	39.7	4.6	3.4	2.6	2.5	1.0	23.0

SOURCE: Field Data

Informants responded to the query on the duration in years since possessing the residential units in which they live. The responses obtained on this are provided in Table 13.7. Accordingly, 27%, 25.4%, 23.7%, 14%, and 7.1% reported that their houses came under their ownership since 20 years or more, 5-9 years, 10-14 years, less than 5 years, and between 15 and 19 years respectively.

Table 13.7: Percentage of respondents by number of rooms in their residential units

			Years since possessed the house				
Woreda	**Town**	**All HHs**	**Less than 5 years**	**5 - 9 years**	**10 - 14 years**	**15 – 19 years**	**20 years or more**
Dembiya	Qoladiba	50	4.0	24.0	10.0	8.0	52.0
Fogera	Woreta	50	24	56.0	16.0	2.0	0.0
Bahr Dar G/Zuria	Bahr Dar	100	19	19.0	19.0	5.0	36.0
	Maksegnit	50	6	32.0	42.0	8.0	10.0
Libo	Addis Zemen	50	16	12.0	12.0	10.0	42.0

Mecha	Merawi	50	12	16.0	48.0	12.0	12.0
Total (All sample towns)		350	14	25.4	23.7	7.1	26.9

SOURCE: Field Data

A number of issues regarding housing conditions and associated facilities were raised in the course of conducting the baseline study in the urban areas in question. Regarding materials used for walls, roofing, and ceilings, data elicited from respondents is indicated in Table 13.8. Regarding materials used for walls, 85 % and 9.4% of the respondents respectively said that wood and mud and hollow block were used. Concerning the roofing of their houses, 95.1% and 0.3% respectively used corrugated iron sheet and concrete cement. Mud, cement concrete, plastic tiles and brick tiles are used for the floors of their houses by 79.4%, 12.9%, 0.3%, and 2.3% of the respondents respectively.

Table 13.8: Percentage of respondents by the type of material used for making wall, roof, floor and ceiling of their house

			Material used for the wall		Material used for the Roof		Material used for floors								
Woreda	Town	All HHs	Wood and mud %	Hollow block %	Corrugated iron sheet	cement Concrete	Mud	Cement concrete	Plastic tiles	Brick tile	Fabrics	Chip wood/ hard board	Wooden	Concrete	Other (madaberia)
Dembiya	Qoladiba	50	96.0	0.0	98.0	0.0	98.0	0	0.0	0.0	0.0	2.0	0.0	0.0	50.0
Fogera	Woreta	50	96	0.0	98.0	0.0	96.0	0	0.0	0.0	0.0	2.0	0.0	0.0	50.0
Bahr Dar	Bahr Dar	100	63	31.0	94.0	1.0	46.0	39	1.0	8.0	13.0	17.0	13.0	1.0	19.0
Gondar Zuria	Maksegnit	50	86	2.0	90.0	0.0	84.0	2	0.0	0.0	2.0	0.0	0.0	0.0	34.0
Libo	Addis Zemen	50	96	2.0	96.0	0.0	96.0	0	0.0	0.0	0.0	0.0	0.0	2.0	24.0
Mecha	Merawi	50	96	0.0	96.0	0.0	90.0	6	0.0	0.0	0.0	2.0	2.0	0.0	46.0
Total (All sample towns)		350	85	9.4	95.1	0.3	79.4	12.29	0.3	2.3	4.0	5.7	4.0	0.6	34.6

SOURCE: Field Data

State of affairs pertaining to facilities like water for various uses, toilet, kitchen etc. characterizing the houses of respondent households is provided in Table 13.9.

Table 13.9: Percentage of respondents by the types of service facilities and amenities available in their house

Woreda	Town	All HHs	Water in Private meter	Shared with others within compound	Water shared with others outside compound	Public Fountain (water)	Shared flush toilet	Dry Pit latrine	shared Bath tub
Dembiya	Qoladiba	50	32.0	0.0	0.0	34.0	40.0	12.0	2.0
Fogera	Woreta	50	82	4.0	0.0	8.0	6.0	0.0	60.0
Bahr Dar	Bahr Dar	100	63	16.0	7.0	2.0	30.0	9.0	30.0
Gondar Zuria	Maksegnit	50	22	0.0	4.0	58.0	0.0	0.0	70.0
Libo	Addis Zemen	50	26	4.0	2.0	60.0	0.0	0.0	66.0
Mecha	Merawi	50	60	4.0	8.0	10.0	10.0	2.0	82.0
Total (All sample towns)		350	0	0.0	0.0		16.6	4.6	48.6

SOURCE: Field Data

Table 13.9 continued

Woreda	Town	All HHs	No kitchen	Modern kitchen private	Modern Kitchen shared	Open drain pipes	None
Dembiya	Qoladiba	50	60.0	0.0	0.0	2.0	94.0
Fogera	Woreta	50	62	6.0	0.0	4.0	92.0
Bahr Dar	Bahr Dar	100	22	15.0	5.0	19.0	44.0
Gondar Zuria	Maksegnit	50	44	0.0	0.0	4.0	58.0
Libo	Addis Zemen	50	50	0.0	2.0	0.0	98.0
Mecha	Merawi	50	0	2.0	0.0	10.0	44.0
Total (All sample towns)		350	37	5.4	1.7	0.0	0.0

SOURCE: Field Data

13.2. House Ownership, Housing Conditions and Facilities

Under this section, informants were asked to provide data on status of ownership of houses, the conditions of residential units in which they dwell and the facilities that are available in the house. Table 13.10 illustrates the status of respondents' ownership of residential units by type in the urban centers and woredas under study. As indicated in the Table, 47% of the total respondents stated that they own non-storied detached residential units. The percentage of those in this category is the highest (98%) in Qoladiba, followed by 75%, 38%, 34%, 8% and 0% in Bahr Dar, Maksegnit, Addis Zemen, Woreta and Merawi respectively. The average percentage of those dwelling in non-storied attached houses is 33.7% of the total of which a maximum of 90% are in Woreta and a minimum of 0% are from Qoladiba and Merawi. On the other hand 100% of the respondents from Merawi reported that they live in mud houses followed by 28% in Maksegnit who were found to be in the same category.

Table 13.10: Percentage of respondents who own houses by type

			Type of House			
Woreda	**Town**	**All HHs**	**% Non-storied detached**	**% Non-storied attached**	**% Other (Mud house)**	**Total**
Dembiya	Qoladiba	50	98.0	0.0	0.0	98.0
Fogera	Woreta	50	8	90.0	0.0	98.0
Bahr Dar	Bahr Dar	100	75	23.0	0.0	98.0
G/Zuria	Maksegnit	50	38	34.0	28.0	100.0
Libo	Addis Zemen	50	34	66.0	0.0	100.0
Mecha	Merawi	50	0	0.0	100.0	100.0
Total (All sample towns)		350	47	33.7	18.3	98.9

SOURCE: Field Data

Data regarding the floor area of residential units owned by respondents in the town under study is provided in Table 13.11. Of the total respondents interviewed in the urban centers under study, the percentage of those who reported the floor area of their houses as being between 25 sq meters and 49 sq meters is over 35.1%. Among these, majorities of 68% and 54% were from Woreta and Addis Zemen respectively. Of the average percentage of 26% the floor area of their houses are less than 25 sq meters, 50% and 40 % were from

Maksegnit and Addis Zemen respectively. On the other hand, the average percentage of respondents with houses on greater than or equal to 75 sq meters is 16.3% of which 44% and 34% are from Merawi and Qoladiba respectively.

Table 13.11: Percentage of respondents who reported owned houses by floor area

			Floor Area (Sq. meter)		
Woreda	**Town**	**All HHs**	**% of HHs with < 25 sq.mts**	**% of HHs with 25-49 sq.mts**	**% of HHs with > =75 sq.mts**
Dembiya	Qoladiba	50	0.0	22.0	34.0
Fogera	Woreta	50	18	68.0	6.0
Bahr Dar	Bahr Dar	100	29	15.0	12.0
G/Zuria	Maksegnit	50	50	46.0	4.0
Libo	Addis Zemen	50	40	54.0	2.0
Mecha	Merawi	50	16	26.0	44.0
Total (All sample towns)		350	26	35.1	16.3

SOURCE: Field Data

Respondents were asked to specify the mode of acquisition and type of tenure under their residential units. Accordingly, it was learnt that 57% of the respondents interviewed in all urban centers under study own the houses in which they live (table 13.12). Of these the majority of 94% were in Woreta followed by 58% and 56% each in Addis Zemen, and Maksegnit and Merawi respectively. The highest percentages of 38% in Qoladiba live in houses rented from kebeles whereas 44% in Merawi live in houses rented from individuals. Only 4% of the informants in Qoladiba stated as living in houses for which they do not pay rent.

Table 13.12: Percentage of respondents who reported house owned by tenure type

			Tenure type				
Woreda	**Town**	**All HHs**	**% Owner occupied**	**% Rented from kebele**	**% Rented from private HHs**	**% Rent-free**	**% Others**
Dembiya	Qoladiba	50	26.0	38.0	28.0	4.0	2.0
Fogera	Woreta	50	94	0.0	6.0	0.0	0.0
Bahr Dar	Bahr Dar	100	53	21.0	25.0	0.0	1.0
G/Zuria	Maksegnit	50	56	2.0	42.0	0.0	0.0
Libo	Addis Zemen	50	58	26.0	16.0	0.0	0.0
Mecha	Merawi	50	56	0.0	44.0	0.0	0.0
Total (All sample towns)		350	57	15.4	26.6	0.6	0.6

SOURCE: Field Data

The percentage of respondents who reported house owned by mode of ownership (purchased/built by own money, purchased/built through bank loan, inherited, gift from relative/friend, aid donation, other) by town and study woreda is provided in Table 13.13. Of a total of 197 informants who reported that they own the houses in which they live, a majority of 78% possessed their residential units through purchasing or building by using own money.

Table 13.13: Percentage of respondents who reported the mode of ownership of houses in which they live

			Mode of ownership				
Woreda	**Town**	**All HHs Who owned ouse**	**% Purchased /built with own money**	**% Purchased /built with bank money**	**% Inher ited**	**% Gift from Relative /friend**	**% Other**
Dembiya	Qoladiba	13	61.5	0.0	15.4	15.4	7.7
Fogera	Woreta	47	93.6	4.3	0.0	2.1	0.0
Bahr Dar	Bahr Dar	53	67.9	3.8	9.4	1.9	17.0
G/Zuria	Maksegnit	28	92.9	0.0	0.0	3.6	3.6
Libo	Addis Zemen	29	93.1	6.9	0.0	0.0	0.0
Mecha	Merawi	27	44.4	0.0	3.7	3.7	48.1
Total (All sample towns)		197	78	3.0	4.1	3.0	12.2

SOURCE: Field Data

The figures in Table 13.14 illustrate the amount of monthly rent that respondents pay for the residential units in which they live. Of the 146 informants who reported that they live in rented houses, an average of 32% pay monthly rents of less than 25 birr whereas 28% incur monthly expenses of about Birr 150 to cover their house rents. The average percentage of those who pay between Birr 25 and 75 for house rent is 15%.

Table 13.14: Percentage of respondents by amount of monthly rent they pay for the house in which they live

			Monthly rent (Birr/ month)			
Woreda	**Town**	**All HHs rented a house**	**% < 25 birr/ month**	**25 – 75 birr/ month**	**75 - 150 birr/month**	**>= 150 birr month**
Dembiya	Qoladiba	33	57.6	18.2	21.2	3.0
Fogera	Woreta	3	0	0.0	33.3	66.7
Bahr Dar	Bahr Dar	45	35.6	17.8	13.3	33.3
G/Zuria	Maksegnit	22	4.55	18.2	40.9	36.4
Libo	Addis Zemen	21	52.4	14.3	28.6	4.8
Mecha	Merawi	22	0	4.5	31.8	63.6
Total (All sample towns)		146	32	15.1	24.7	28.1

SOURCE: Field Data

The percentage of respondents who reported the number of rooms in their houses is provided in Table 13.15. Of the total of 350 respondents in all the urban centers under study, an average percentage of 50% lives in residential units having between 1 and 2 rooms. Of these, the great majority of 82% are in Qoladiba, followed by 78% and 62% in Addis Zemen and Maksegnit respectively. The average percentage of those living in houses with 3-4 rooms is 39.7% of which 72% are from Woreta.

Table 13.15: Percentage of respondents by number of rooms in their residential units

			Number of rooms per household							
Woreda	**Town**	**All HHs**	**% of HHs with 1 - 2 rooms**	**% of HHs with 3 - 4 rooms**	**% of HHs with 5 - 6 rooms**	**% of HHs with >= 7 rooms**	**Mean**	**Median**	**Min**	**Max**
Dembiya	Qoladiba	50	82.0	16.0	0.0	0.0	1.6	1.0	1.0	4.0
Fogera	Woreta	50	28	72.0	0.0	0.0	2.8	3.0	1.0	4.0
Bahr Dar	Bahr Dar	100	38	29.0	14.0	12.0	4.0	3.0	1.0	23.0
G/Zuria	Maksegnit	50	62	38.0	0.0	0.0	2.2	2.0	1.0	3.0
Libo	Addis Zemen	50	78	22.0	0.0	0.0	2.0	2.0	1.0	3.0
Mecha	Merawi	50	24	72.0	4.0	0.0	2.9	3.0	1.0	5.0
Total (All sample towns)		350	50	39.7	4.6	3.4	2.6	2.5	1.0	23.0

SOURCE: Field Data

Informants responded to the query on the duration in years since possessing the residential units in which they live. The responses obtained on this are provided in Table 13.16. Accordingly, 27%, 25.4%, 23.7%, 14%, and 7.1% reported that their houses came under their ownership since 20 years or more, 5-9 years, 10-14 years, less than 5 years, and between 15 and 19 years respectively.

Table 13.16: Percentage of respondents by number of rooms in their residential units

			Years since possessed the house				
Woreda	**Town**	**All HHs**	**Less than 5 years**	**5 – 9 years**	**10 – 14 years**	**15 – 19 years**	**20 years or more**
Dembiya	Qoladiba	50	4.0	24.0	10.0	8.0	52.0
Fogera	Woreta	50	24	56.0	16.0	2.0	0.0
Bahr Dar	Bahr Dar	100	19	19.0	19.0	5.0	36.0
G/Zuria	Maksegnit	50	6	32.0	42.0	8.0	10.0
Libo	Addis Zemen	50	16	12.0	12.0	10.0	42.0
Mecha	Merawi	50	12	16.0	48.0	12.0	12.0
Total (All sample towns)		350	14	25.4	23.7	7.1	26.9

SOURCE: Field Data

A number of issues regarding housing conditions and associated facilities were raised in the course of conducting the baseline study in the urban areas in question. Regarding materials used for walls, roofing, and ceilings, data elicited from respondents is indicated in Table 13.17. Regarding materials used for walls, 85 % and 9.4% of the respondents respectively said that wood and mud and hollow block were used. Concerning the roofing of their houses, 95.1% and 0.3% respectively used corrugated iron sheet and concrete cement. Mud, cement concrete, plastic tiles and brick tiles are used for the floors of their houses by 79.4%, 12.9%, 0.3%, and 2.3% of the respondents respectively.

Table 13.17: Percentage of respondents by the type of material used for making wall, roof, floor and ceiling of their house

			Material used for the wall		Material used for the Roof		Material used for floors								
Woreda	Town	All HHs	Wood and mud %	Hollow block %	Corrugated Iron sheet	cement Concrete	Mud	Cement concrete	Plastic tiles	Brick tile	Fabrics	Chip wood/ hard board	Wooden	Concrete	Other (madaberia)
Dembiya	Qoladiba	50	96.0	0.0	98.0	0.0	98.0	0	0.0	0.0	0.0	2.0	0.0	0.0	50.0
Fogera	Woreta	50	96	0.0	98.0	0.0	96.0	0	0.0	0.0	0.0	2.0	0.0	0.0	50.0
Bahr Dar	Bahr Dar	100	63	31.0	94.0	1.0	46.0	39	1.0	8.0	13.0	17.0	13.0	1.0	19.0
Gondar Zuria	Maksegnit	50	86	2.0	90.0	0.0	84.0	2	0.0	0.0	2.0	0.0	0.0	0.0	34.0
Libo	Addis Zemen	50	96	2.0	96.0	0.0	96.0	0	0.0	0.0	0.0	0.0	0.0	2.0	24.0
Mecha	Merawi	50	96	0.0	96.0	0.0	90.0	6	0.0	0.0	0.0	2.0	2.0	0.0	46.0
Total (All sample towns)		350	85	9.4	95.1	0.3	79.4	12.29	0.3	2.3	4.0	5.7	4.0	0.6	34.6

SOURCE: Field Data

State of affairs pertaining to facilities like water for various uses, toilet, kitchen etc. characterizing the houses of respondent households is provided in Table 13.18.

Table 13.18: Percentage of respondents by the types of service facilities and amenities available in their house

						Toilet			
Woreda	**Town**	**All HHs**	**Water in Private meter**	**Shared with Other within compound**	**Water shared with others outside compound**	**Public Fountain (water)**	**Shared flush toilet**	**Dry pit latrine**	**shared Bath tub**
Dembiya	Qoladiba	50	32.0	0.0	0.0	34.0	40.0	12.0	2.0
Fogera	Woreta	50	82	4.0	0.0	8.0	6.0	0.0	60.0
Bahr Dar	Bahr Dar	100	63	16.0	7.0	2.0	30.0	9.0	30.0
Gondar Zuria	Maksegnit	50	22	0.0	4.0	58.0	0.0	0.0	70.0
Libo	Addis Zemen	50	26	4.0	2.0	60.0	0.0	0.0	66.0
Mecha	Merawi	50	60	4.0	8.0	10.0	10.0	2.0	82.0
Total (All sample towns)		350	0	0.0	0.0		16.6	4.6	48.6

SOURCE: Field Data

Woreda	**Town**	**All HHs**	**No kitchen**	**Modern kitchen private**	**Modern kitchen shared**	**Open drain pipes**	**None**
Dembiya	Qoladiba	50	60.0	0.0	0.0	2.0	94.0
Fogera	Woreta	50	62	6.0	0.0	4.0	92.0
Bahr Dar	Bahr Dar	100	22	15.0	5.0	19.0	44.0
Gondar Zuria	Maksegnit	50	44	0.0	0.0	4.0	58.0
Libo	Addis Zemen	50	50	0.0	2.0	0.0	98.0
Mecha	Merawi	50	0	2.0	0.0	10.0	44.0
Total (All sample towns)		350	37	5.4	1.7	0.0	0.0

SOURCE: Field Data

XIV. HEALTH

The overall situation pertaining to health matters in the urban centers under study is the focus of discussion in this section.

14.1 Recurrent Diseases

Informants were asked to provide information on the state of recurrent diseases affecting members of respondent households by specifying the types of health hazards (Table 14.1). An average of nearly 43% of the respondents reported that household members in the urban centers under study are affected by other diseases that are not listed here. Of these 100% each from Maksegnit and Addis Zemen, followed by 84.6%, 80%, and 62.5% in Qoladiba, Woreta, and Merawi were respectively affected. An average of 19%, 16.7%, 15.5%, and 6% stated that household members were affected by ailments caused by malaria, typhus, cough, and tuberculosis respectively.

Table 14.1: Percentage of respondents who reported recurrent disease affecting hhs by type

				Households recurrently affected by disease				
Woreda	**Town**	**All HHs**	**% of HHs affected**	**% Cough**	**% TB**	**% Malaria**	**% Typhus**	**% Other disease**
Dembiya	Qoladiba	50	26.0	0.0	7.7	7.7	0.0	84.6
Fogera	Woreta	50	10	0.0	20.0	0.0	0.0	80.0
Bahr Dar	Bahr Dar	100	49	26.5	4.1	26.5	28.6	14.3
G/Zuria	Maksegnit	50	12	0.0	0.0	0.0	0.0	100.0
Libo	Addis Zemen	50	6	0.0	0.0	0.0	0.0	100.0
Mecha	Merawi	50	16	0.0	12.5	25.0	0.0	62.5
Total (All sample towns)		350	24	15.5	6.0	19.0	16.7	42.9

SOURCE: field data

14.2. Status of Family Health

Regarding the query on the status of family health of members of households of informants, the responses elicited are provided in Table 14.2. As shown in the

Table, an average of 15% reported that the status of their family members' is excellent whereas nearly 49% and 29% reported this as being very good and good respectively. Those who said that the situation of health of family members is poor is nearly 7% of the total on the average.

Table 14.2: Percentage of respondents who reported family health by status

			Family health status			
Woreda	**Town**	**All HHs**	**% Excellent**	**% Very good**	**% Good**	**% Poor**
Dembiya	Qoladiba	50	2.0	34.0	42.0	20.0
Fogera	Woreta	50	36	52.0	10.0	2.0
Bahr Dar	Bahr Dar	100	7	39.0	44.0	10.0
G/Zuria	Maksegnit	50	4	68.0	22.0	4.0
Libo	Addis Zemen	50	12	62.0	24.0	0.0
Mecha	Merawi	50	34	48.0	14.0	2.0
Total (All sample towns)		350	15	48.9	28.6	6.9

SOURCE: field data

14.3. Family Members' Loss of Life by Cause

Informants were asked to provide information whether they have encountered loss of life of family members in the last 5 years by indicating causes of such occurrence. Elicited responses regarding this are provided in Table 14.3. Accordingly, an average of 3.1% of the respondents in the study towns stated that they have lost family members due to a variety of causes in the last 5 years. Of these 45.5% reported that the mishap took place due to abortion. Among those that reported the incident, all informants from Woreta and Addis Zemen attributed the incident to abortion. This is followed by an average of 27.3% mentioning other causes of death. The average percentage of informants who reported death of family members due to lack of proper maternal care is 9% of which 33.3% took place in Merawi.

Table 14.3: Percentage of respondents who reported family members' death in the last 5 years by cause

			Households reported death in the last 5 years			
Woreda	**Town**	**All HHs**	**% of HHs Reported death**	**% Lack of proper Maternal care**	**% Attempted abortion**	**% Other**
Dembiya	Qoladiba	50	0.0	-	-	-
Fogera	Woreta	50	4.0	0.0	100.0	0.0
Bahr Dar	Bahr Dar	100	2.0	0.0	0.0	50.0
G/Zuria	Maksegnit	50	2.0	0.0	0.0	0.0
Libo	Addis Zemen	50	6.0	0.0	100.0	0.0
Mecha	Merawi	50	6.0	33.3	0.0	66.7
Total (All sample towns)		350	3.1	9.1	45.5	27.3

SOURCE: field data

14.4. Medical Care

The study has made inquiries regarding the percentage of households whose members have sought medical care in the last three months from various providers preceding the conducting of the baseline survey. The percentage of responses elicited in this regard is provided in Table 14.4. Of the total, 53.4% reported that members of their households sought medical treatment during the period in question. Of these, 70%, 68% and 66% were from Merawi, Qoladiba and Bahr Dar respectively. The average percentage of those who visited traditional facilities to this end is less than 1% whereas nearly 45% reported that they went to modern providers like health posts, health centers and clinics of which the highest percentages of 72% and 70% were recorded in Maksegnit and Addis Zemen respectively.

Table 14.4: Percentage of respondents who sought medical care by service providers

Woreda	Town	All HHs	% hhs sought treatment	% Went to traditional facilities	% Went to clinics, HP or HCs
Dembiya	Qoladiba	50	68.0	0.0	30.0
Fogera	Woreta	50	50.0	0.0	50.0
Bahr Dar	Bahr Dar	100	66.0	0.0	33.0
G/Zuria	Maksegnit	50	24.0	4.0	72.0
Libo	Addis Zemen	50	30.0	0.0	70.0
Mecha	Merawi	50	70.0	2.0	24.0
Total (All sample towns)		350	53.4	0.9	44.6

SOURCE: field data

14.5. Consumption of Meals by HHs

Respondents were asked to indicate the frequency and average number of meals consumed by members of their households per day (Table 14.5). As shown in the figures in the table, only 2% of the respondents in Bahr Dar stated that members of their households take only one meal per day. Among those who stated that household members consume 2 meals per day, 13% were from Bahr Dar, 12% from Addis Zemen, 8% each from Maksegnit and Merawi, and 4% from Woreta. An average percentage of 83.4% was recorded for all study sites where household members consume three meals per day. All in all, the average number of meals consumed by household members in all locations under study is 2.9.

Table 14.5: Percentage of Respondents by number of meals/hh/day

Woreda	Town	All HHs	One Meal %	Two Meals %	Three Meals %	Average number meals/day
Dembiya	Qoladiba	50	0.0	0.0	100.0	3.0
Fogera	Woreta	50	0	4.0	86.0	3.0
Bahr Dar	Bahr Dar	100	2	13.0	77.0	2.9
Gondar Zuria	Maksegnit	50	0	8.0	82.0	2.9
Libo	Addis Zemen	50	0	12.0	78.0	2.9
Mecha	Merawi	50	0	8.0	84.0	3.0
Total (All sample towns)		350	1	8.3	83.4	2.9

SOURCE: field data

Data on the frequency of consumption of meat by members of respondent households is provided in Table 14.6. A majority of nearly 65% of the respondents stated that their families consume meat on holidays whereas 9%, 11.4%, and 10.6% respectively reported that this takes once or more per week, once in two weeks, and once a month.

Table 14.6: Percentage of respondents who reported consumption of meat by frequency

			Frequency of Meat consumption of HHs					
Woreda	**Town**	**All HHs**	**% More than once in a week**	**% Once in two weeks**	**% Once in a month**	**% on holidays**	**% never**
Dembiya	Qoladiba	50	30.0	40.0	22.0	4.0	0.0
Fogera	Woreta	50	0.0	0.0	2.0	96.0	0.0
Bahr Dar	Bahr Dar	100	14.0	12.0	5.0	63.0	3.0
G/Zuria	Maksegnit	50	0.0	4.0	14.0	82.0	0.0
Libo	Addis Zemen	50	0.0	2.0	8.0	80.0	0.0
Mecha	Merawi	50	4.0	10.0	18.0	66.0	0.0
Total (All sample towns)		350	8.9	11.4	10.6	64.9	0.9

SOURCE: field data

XV. EXPENDITURE AND LINKAGE

15.1 Household expenditure

Households expend for different purposes. The majority (87%) responded that they expend for cloth purchase and 72% mentioned they have transport expenditure (Table 15.1). Transport expenditure is reported by higher number of respondents in Bahr Dar. Education and health expenditure are also mentioned by 61% and 63% of the respondents respectively. Expenditure for wedding and memorial feasts which happen occasionally is reported by a fewer proportion of households. The annual average expenditure for clothing (1539 birr) is higher than the amount for other expenditures (Table 15.2). The second and third most important expenditure items in terms of amount expended are education (985 birr) and wedding (857 birr). In terms of towns, households in Bahr Dar seem to have higher amount of average expenditure while households in Qoladiba and Addis Zemen have lower amount of average expenditure.

Table 15.3 shows the purchasing place of household form the major expenditure items. The table indicates that most of the items (cloth, health, education, tax) are expended in the same locality. It is only a few households who visit other towns to source the items listed above. Expenditure on major items therefore cannot be used as bases for inter-urban linkage in the study area. Table 15.4 shows the household consumption for a period of two weeks. The major consumption goods reported by many households in all the study towns are oil (288), vegetable (276), sugar (271), tea (265), and soap (235). The amount expended in these items is 69 birr for oil, 37 birr for vegetable, 42 birr for sugar, and 25 birr for soap. The least consumed items are rice, pasta and tobacco. These items however have relatively higher expenditure.

Table 15.1: Percent distribution of household who reported expenditure

			Percent household who reported expenditure								
Woreda	**Town**	**All hhs**	**Cloth %**	**Education %**	**Health %**	**tax %**	**Wedding %**	**Memorial feast %**	**Church /Mosque %**	**Transport %**	**other %**
Dembiya	Qoladiba	50	80	54	58	32	32	20	42	44	0
Fogera	Woreta	50	94	86	58	82	2	2	24	68	0
Bahr Dar	Bahr Dar	100	88	71	69	52	11	55	75	88	9
G/Zuria	Maksegnit	50	86	40	70	32	2	4	40	74	0
Libo	Addis Zemen	50	86	34	54	32	2	0	26	58	0
Mecha	Merawi	50	88	70	60	60	8	2	76	82	0
	total	350	87.1	60.9	62.6	48.9	9.7	19.7	51.1	71.7	2.6

SOURCE: Field Data

Table 15.2: Mean amount of household expenditure on different items for reporting households (birr)

Woreda	**Town**	**clothing and foot wear**	**Education**	**Health**	**Tax**	**Wedding**	**Memorial feast**	**Church/ Mosque**	**Transport**	**Other**
Dembiya	Qoladiba	943.1	118.0	218.07	1017.1	125	1120	217.0	332.4	0
Fogera	Woreta	1171.9	461.2	496.41	400.0	2000	0	43.5	499.6	0
Bahr Dar	Bahr Dar	2597.1	1454.8	1282	828.5	463.6	511	315.0	849.6	2316
G/Zuria	Maksegnit	934.9	568.7	507.86	422.8	2000	50	42.6	417.3	0
Libo	Addis Zemen	952.0	155.4	664.19	172.6	30	0	102.0	551.7	0
Mecha	Merawi	1517.0	1987.1	682.5	949.1	4500	0	439.7	668.8	0

Total (All sample towns)	1538.5	985.3	755.08	665.2	856.8	571	265.9	629.2	2316

SOURCE: Field Data

Table 15.3: Percent household reporting purchase places for cloth, education, health and tax

			Percent households reporting purchase place			
Cloth		**reporting hhs**	**rural area (%)**	**woreda capital (%)**	**other town (%)**	**Bahr Dar (%)**
Dembiya	Qoladiba	40	0	85	15	0
Fogera	Woreta	47	0	100	0	0
Bahr Dar	Bahr Dar	85	0	4.7	1.2	94.1
G/Zuria	Maksegnit	43	0	86.0	11.6	2.3
Libo	Addis Zemen	44	0	97.7	2.3	0
Mecha	Merawi	44	0	79.6	4.5	15.9
Total		303	0	66.0	4.9	29
Education						
Dembiya	Qoladiba	27	0	96.3	3.7	0
Fogera	Woreta	41	0	95.1	4.9	0
Bahr Dar	Bahr Dar	69	1.5	2.9	0	95.7
G/Zuria	Maksegnit	20	0	85	10	5
Libo	Addis Zemen	17	0	100	0	0
Mecha	Merawi	35	0	94.3	2.9	2.9
Total		209	0.5	64.1	2.9	32.5

Health						
Dembiya	Qoladiba	29	0	93.1	6.9	0
Fogera	Woreta	28	0	85.7	0	14.3
	Bahr Dar	66	1.5	1.5	1.5	95.5
G/Zuria	Maksegnit	35	0	80	17.1	2.9
Libo	Addis Zemen	26	0	84.62	7.6	7.7
Mecha	Merawi	30	0	73.33	3.3	23.3
Total		214	0.5	57.94	5.6	36
Tax						
Dembiya	Qoladiba	15	0	100	0	0
Fogera	Woreta	33	3.0	96.97	0	0
Bahr Dar	Bahr Dar	51	1.9	0	0	98
G/Zuria	Maksegnit	16	0	93.75	0	6.25
Libo	Addis Zemen	15	0	100	0	0
Mecha	Merawi	28	0	100	0	0
Total		**158**	**1.3**	**66.46**	**0**	**32.3**

SOURCE: Field Data

Table 15.4: Number of Household who purchased consumption goods and mean expenditure amount in the last two weeks

	Qoladiba		Woreta		Bahr Dar		Maksegnit		Addis Zemen		Merawi		Total	
	HH who purchased	**Mean amount**	**HH who purchased**	**Mean amount**	**HH who purchased**	**Mean amount**	**HH who purchased**	**Mean amount**	**HH who purchased**	**Mean amount**	**HH who purchased**	**Mean amount**	**HH who purchased**	**mean**
Grain/ Flour	21	327	2	13	63	904	8	163	1	24	14	405	109	650.2
Rice	2	17.5	5	43.2	22	80.4	4	19.2	3	15.5	9	22	45	52
Pasta	1	15	6	14.6	45	54.6	4	36.3	5	30	12	31	73	44.2
Sugar	37	22.2	45	27.5	84	75.3	33	25.6	32	19.7	40	41	271	42.5
Tea	43	39.9	36	32.7	62	102.8	38	37.2	43	27.8	43	48	265	52.7
Match	13	4.07	7	4	52	3.66	29	9.05	15	25.7	43	11	159	8.78
Oil	45	52.1	44	68.1	75	110.1	40	52.8	39	42.8	45	56	288	69.1
Beans	17	29	10	41	17	189.9	8	46.5	5	35.8	11	119	68	88.12
Vegetable	49	23.8	27	28.5	80	56.5	38	24.4	36	25.9	46	39	276	36.6
Meat	33	75.6	42	204.1	48	391.1	25	126	26	152.3	41	242	215	218
Tobacco	1	70	5	740	3	36.6	6	401	12	102	0	0	27	278.3
Soap	32	19.1	25	15.7	82	35.8	28	21.8	23	18.4	43	23	235	25.6
Kerosene	0	0	1	3	7	279	1	9	0	0	9	12	18	115.3
Total	**47**	**365**	**38**	**4334**	**93**	**1134**	**45**	**292**	**48**	**221.2**	**48**	532	319	590.6

SOURCE: Field Data

15.2 Linkage with rural areas

15.2.1 Investment linkage

One of the ways town people link with rural people is through investment. About 14 % of the households have indicated that they invest in rural areas (Table 15.5). It can also be seen that Woreta with 56% of the households reporting investment in rural areas is the town that is most linked with rural areas. The reason is that Woreta has high irrigated land and urban households rent land for purposes of growing crops. This indicates that rural potential is a significant factor for forging strong linkage with rural areas. The main type of investment is investment on farm. The amount of investment ranges from a minimum of 200 birr to 37,600 birr with the average amount of investment being 5900 birr.

Table 15.6 shows the constraints urban households face in investing in rural areas. As it is shown in the table, lack of access to land (62.3%) is the major constraint that hinders investing in rural areas. Land in rural area can be possessed by rural dwellers and hence there is no provision for urban households to own land. The only way for urban households to engage in farming is through land rental. The second major constraint identified by respondents is shortage of money (23.1%). This is an indication that households with no financial capacity cannot invest in rural areas.

15.2.2 Market linkage

Table 15.7 shows the extent of market linkage urban households exhibit with rural areas through purchases of rural products. Livestock, livestock products and grains are chosen as rural products that can be purchased by urban households. The responses indicate that the majority of the respondents purchase the three items from the same town they live. A very negligible proportion of households purchase these items from the surrounding rural areas.

Table 15.8 shows that urban dwellers mainly purchase livestock (67%), livestock products (66.3%) and grains (38.6%) directly from farmers. About 53% of the households however indicate that traders are their main suppliers of grains. It thus appears that traders bring grains from rural areas and farmers visit towns to sell their livestock and livestock products. This shows that in the marketing linkage of urban households, farmers and traders play a significant role.

Table 15.5: Investment in rural areas

		Households who invested in rural areas			Type of investment		Amount of investment			
Woreda	**Town**	**All HHs**	**Frequency**	**%**	**investment on farm (%)**	**Other (%)**	**Minimum (Birr)**	**Maximum (Birr)**	**Total Sum (Birr)**	**Mean amount (Birr)**
Dembiya	Qoladiba	50	2	4.0	0.0	4.0	250.0	300	550	275
Fogera	Woreta	50	28	56.0	56.0	0.0	200.0	37600.0	190845.0	6815.8
Bahr Dar	Bahr Dar	100	1	3.0	1.0	2.0	12000.0	12000.0	12000.0	12,000
G/Zuria	Maksegnit	50	4	10.0	8.0	4.0	600.0	6300.0	9450.0	2362.5
Libo	Addis Zemen	50	2	10.0	4.0	6.0	1120.0	6000.0	7120.0	3560
Mecha	Merawi	50	5	12.0	10.0	2.0	2000.0	5000.0	16600.0	3320
Total (All sample towns)		**350**	**40**	**14.0**	**11.4**	**2.9**	**200.0**	**37600.0**	**236015.0**	**5900.3**

SOURCE: Field Data

Table 15.6: Difficulties in investing in rural areas

Woreda	**Town**	**% access to land is difficult (%)**	**% rural activities are not profitable (%)**	**% No activities worth Investing (%)**	**shortage of money (%)**
Dembiya	Qoladiba	2.0	2	2	94
Fogera	Woreta	72.0	6	8	0
Bahr Dar	Bahr Dar	42.0	3	9	33
G/Zuria	Maksegnit	90.0	0	0	0
Libo	Addis Zemen	96.0	0	0	0

Mecha	Merawi	92.0	2	0	2
Total		**62.3**	**2.2**	**4**	**23.1**

SOURCE: Field Data

Table 15.7: Urban households' purchasing places of rural products

			Livestock			**Livestock products**			**Grains**		
Woreda	**Town**	**All HHs**	**The same town (%)**	**The surrounding rural areas (%)**	**Another town**	**The same town (%)**	**Surrounding rural areas (%)**	**Other town (%)**	**The same town (%)**	**Surrounding town (%)**	**Other town (%)**
Dembiya	Qoladiba	50	98.0	2.0	0.0	98.0	0.0	2.0	98.0	0.0	0.0
Fogera	Woreta	50	94.0	0.0	0.0	92.0	0.0	0.0	88.0	0.0	2.0
Bahr Dar	Bahr Dar	100	65.0	0.0	0.0	75.0	0.0	0.0	94.0	0.0	0.0
G/Zuria	Maksegnit	50	90.0	0.0	0.0	90.0	0.0	0.0	88.0	0.0	2.0
Libo	Addis Zemen	50	98.0	0.0	0.0	98.0	0.0	0.0	98.0	0.0	0.0
Mecha	Merawi	50	68.0	0.0	0.0	76.0	0.0	6.0	84.0	0.0	8.0
Total (All sample towns)		**350**	**82.6**	**0.3**	**0.0**	**86.3**	**0.0**	**1.1**	**92.0**	**0.0**	**1.7**

SOURCE: Field Data

Table 15.8: Percentage of households by type of dealers/individuals and towns from whom urban households purchase rural items.

			Livestock				Livestock products				Grains			
Woreda	Town	All HHs	Directly From farmers	Traders	Middle men	No answer	Farmers	Traders	Middle men	No answer	Farmers	Traders	Middle men	No answer
Dembiya	Qoladiba	50	86.0	14.0	0.0	0.0	70.0	28.0	2.0	0.0	34.0	64.0	0.0	2.0
Fogera	Woreta	50	94.0	2.0	0.0	4.0	88.0	4.0	0.0	8.0	34.0	56.0	0.0	10.0
Bahr Dar	Bahr Dar	100	25.0	40.0	0.0	35.0	28.0	47.0	0.0	25.0	9.0	83.0	1.0	8.0
G/Zuria	Maksegnit	50	84.0	6.0	0.0	10.0	84.0	6.0	0.0	10.0	52.0	38.0	0.0	10.0
Libo	Addis Zemen	50	94.0	0.0	0.0	6.0	96.0	0.0	0.0	4.0	52.0	44.0	0.0	4.0
Mecha	Merawi	50	62.0	6.0	0.0	32.0	70.0	8.0	2.0	20.0	80.0	6.0	2.0	12.0
Total (All sample towns)		**350**	**67.1**	**15.4**	**0.0**	**17.5**	**66.3**	**20.0**	**0.6**	**12.9**	**38.6**	**53.4**	**0.6**	**7.4**

SOURCE: Field Data

XVI. FOOD STATUS, COPING STRATEGIES AND WELL BEING

16.1 Food status

Table 16.1 shows that about 9% of the households reported food shortages. Respondents in Qoladiba, Bahr Dar and Addis Zemen relatively have higher proportion of households (12%) who reported food shortage. The minimum number of months when households face food shortage ranges from one to eight. Eight months of food shortages is reported by some households in Bahr Dar. The mean number of months with food shortages for all households is 3.2 months. The mean number is relatively higher in Bahr Dar with 4.4 months. Food shortage though not a critical problem in all the study towns, still needs some attention for those facing the problem

Table 16.1: Household food status

			Food status of households			
Woreda	**Town**	**All H Hs**	**% HHs facing Food shortage**	**Mean no. of months of food shortage**	**Ministry of months of food shortage**	**maximum of months of food shortage**
Dembiya	Qoladiba	50	12.0	2.8	2.0	3.0
Fogera	Woreta	50	4.0	1.5	1.0	2.0
Bahr Dar G/Zuria	Bahr Dar	10 0	12.0	4.4	1.0	8.0
	Maksegnit	50	6.0	2.5	2.0	3.0
Libo	Addis Zemen	50	12.0	2.0	1.0	4.0
Mecha	Merawi	50	2.0	3.0	3.0	3.0
Total (All sample towns)		**35 0**	**8.6**	**3.2**	**1.0**	**8.0**

SOURCE: Field Data

16.2 Coping strategies

The coping strategies of households when faced with food shortages are indicated in table 16.2. These strategies indicate what households will do if and when faced by food shortage. Labor employment (54.3%) is the primary coping strategy to make up for food shortages. This is followed by borrowing (39.1%) and selling household assets (29.4%) as the second and third important forms of coping strategies. It is however interesting to note that there is a significant variation among towns. For instance, donation and food for work each are reported by 88% of households in Merawi. Borrowing is significant in Qoladiba (92%) while labor employment is the preferred strategy by the majority of respondents in Woreta, Bahr Dar, Maksegnit and Addis Zemen. It is also interesting to note that respondents in Bahr Dar have a more diverse set of preferred strategy compared to other towns.

16.3 Households' wellbeing

Table 16.3 is households' own evaluation of own income, food consumption and clothing adequacy as measures of well being. The table indicates that 51% of the households believe that their income is not adequate and 21 % believe their food consumption is not adequate and 34% believe they have inadequate clothing. Income therefore is the most problematic area for most households' well being. Inadequate income obviously will translate into poor or inadequate consumption, poor saving and poor investment. The fact that only 21 % reported inadequate food consumption indicates that households in the study area do not suffer from food shortage. This is in line with table 8.1 above which showed only 9% of the households suffering from food shortages. In terms of households in each town, households in Addis Zemen, Makes ignite and Qoladiba have more households who reported shortage of income. Similarly Maksegnit and Addis Zemen have more number of households suffering from inadequate food consumption and inadequate clothing. It can thus be inferred that Addis Zemen, Maksegnit and Qoladiba have more households with lower well being status than households in Woreta, Bahr Dar and Merawi.

Table 16.2: Coping strategies of households when faced with food shortages

Town	Total sample	% Labor employ ment	% Selling house hold assets	% Selling productive assets	% Renting house	% Borrowi ng	% Donatio n	% Begging	% Migr ation	% Food for work	% Sell straw	% Other strate gies
Qoladiba	50	32.0	14.0	16.0	4.0	92.0	4.0	0.0	0.0	0.0	0.0	4.0
Woreta	50	62.0	22.0	2.0	0.0	22.0	0.0	0.0	4.0	4.0	0.0	0.0
Bahr Dar	100	51.0	40.0	11.0	31.0	30.0	11.0	6.0	21.0	26.0	2.0	3.0
Maksegnit	50	52.0	36.0	2.0	4.0	26.0	2.0	0.0	6.0	22.0	0.0	4.0
Addis Zemen	50	66.0	18.0	0.0	6.0	16.0	0.0	0.0	0.0	0.0	0.0	0.0
Merawi	50	66.0	36.0	26.0	34.0	58.0	88.0	0.0	4.0	80.0	2.0	0.0
Total	**350**	**54.3**	**29.4**	**9.7**	**15.7**	**39.1**	**16.6**	**1.7**	**8.0**	**22.6**	**0.9**	**2.0**

SOURCE: Field Data

Table 16.3: Household evaluation of own income, food consumption and clothing adequacy

Town		Number of reporting households	Not adequate	Adequate	More than adequate
Qoladiba	Household income over the past one month	50	50	50	0
	Household food consumption over the past one month	50	20	78	2
	Household clothing	50	28	72	0
Woreta	Household income over the past one month	49	38.7	59.2	2.0
	Household food consumption over the past one month	49	4.1	95.9	0

	Household clothing	49	8.2	85.7	6.1
Bahr Dar	Household income over the past one month	95	36.8	61.1	2.1
	Household food consumption over the past one month	95	13.6	83.1	3.1
	Household clothing	95	27.3	65.3	7.4
Maksegnit	Household income over the past one month	45	75.5	24.4	0
	Household food consumption over the past one month	45	40	60	0
	Household clothing	45	55.5	44.4	0
Addis Zemen	Household income over the past one month	49	75.5	24.5	0
	Household food consumption over the past one month	49	32.6	67.3	0
	Household clothing	49	65.3	34.6	0
Merawi	Household income over the past one month	48	41.6	58.3	0
	Household food consumption over the past one month	48	22.9	77.1	0
	Household clothing	46	23.9	76.1	0
Total	**Household income over the past one month**	**336**	**50.5**	**48.5**	**0.8**
	Household food consumption over the past one month	**336**	**20.8**	**77.9**	**1.1**
	Household clothing	**334**	**33.5**	**63.5**	**2.9**

SOURCE: Field Data

XVII. RECOMMENDATIONS FOR FUTURE RESEARCH

The purpose of this study is to provide a base line data that could be used to monitor changes and assess the impact of development interventions in the study *woredas* and urban centers. In this regard, the study has captured the socio-economic situation of the rural and urban households with respect to household composition, the practice of agriculture, assets, housing, health, non-farm activities, food status, migration, employment, income and business, access to services, assets, expenditure and linkage. In addition to this, the following provides some recommendations of research ideas in light of the findings of the study that might be worth investigating in the study *woredas* and towns.

1. *Rural illiteracy*: The study has found that 48% or nearly half of the population aged 6 years and over are illiterate. Given such high level of illiteracy, how does illiteracy affect the production system of the *woredas* that have been studied? Are farmers receptive to modern techniques of agriculture or how do farmers seek information on inputs, prices, markets etc. in the sampled *woredas* need to be studied.

2. *Landlessness among the youth:* The study has revealed that the youth (aged 21-30) has limited ownership of land for farming or in other words landlessness is acute among the youth in the *woredas* studied. One of the reasons for such high incidence of landlessness among the youth could be the paucity of land in the area. On the other hand, the youth require a means of sustenance in rural areas. It might, therefore, be worth investigating the causes and consequences of youth land-lessness and the alternatives means of livelihoods to sustain the youth. In the same way, those in the old age do not possess land. This also begs some further inquiry into how the old can be accommodated in different life sustenance means, including safety net and other social protection programs.

3. *Agricultural production:* Data elicited in regard to annual agricultural production in the study woredas indicate that there is variation between production during spring and main harvest seasons. Accordingly, it was reported that mean production per hectare stands at 6.7 quintals and 28.3 quintals in 2004 EC during spring and main harvest seasons respectively. It was learnt that during the year in question, average production was between a minimum of 17.4 quintals/ha and a maximum of 44.7 quintals/ha. Informants are of the view that variability in production per hectare is attributed to adequacy of rainfall, application of improved inputs, and quality of seed. It could thus be argued that optimal increase in the amount of production can be realized , among others, through

recourse to irrigation by intensifying water harvesting and conservation and augmented use of agricultural inputs where the practice is minimal in the localities where reduced production is experienced. Hence it is expected that subsequent studies will focus on those offsetting the aforementioned inadequacies.

4. *Land renting*: Land renting is a significant means of acquiring land in the rural *woredas* covered in this study. About 158 individuals or 32% acquire land through renting. It might be useful to make an in-depth study of land renting arrangements, including the socio-economic characteristics of persons who rent in and rent out land and the consequences of renting for those who rent in and rent out land

5. *Tenure security and land certificate*: The overwhelming proportion of the respondents (94%) in the rural areas has stated that they have security of tenure. Similarly 89% have received land certificates. It might therefore be interesting to know the relation between land certificates and tenure security. It is also interesting to understand the effects of tenure security on improving productivity, land protection, etc. in the areas studied. In addition, it is hoped that subsequent studies would shed light whether the project has contributed to improvement in enjoyment of use rights covering the entire farming households in the study areas .

6. *Landlesseness of adults and land fragmentation*: It was found out that each respondent household owns 1.3 hectares of land on the average. Though this is significant as compared to the situation in most parts of the highlands of the country where the average holding is often less than 1 hectare, a progressively growing incidence of landlessness in the localities under study is alarming. According to the findings of the study, the percentage of people with no land within the age range of 31 and 50 lies between a minimum of 35% in Mecha and 51% in Fogera, which appears to be considerable whereas farming households between the age range of 51-70 suffering from lack of land is around a minimum of 69% in Fogera and 92% in Mecha and Dembiya. In the latter case in particular, catering for the needs of the aged would be increasingly difficult given that the majority of old people in the study areas do not have land, which is a major means of livelihood in rural Ethiopia. Moreover, fragmentation of plots affecting those who own land is observed in the study areas where the majority has between 3 to 5 different plots depriving people from enjoying the benefits of economy of scale. It could thus be envisaged that subsequent studies may establish whether the project has brought about positive ramifications in generating gainful non-farm employment opportunities for the landless and land consolidation schemes that bring

together the fragmented plots including interventions promoting social welfare for the aged and other vulnerable groups in the intervention areas.

7. *Hired labor*: Use of hired labor is prevalent in the study woredas. It was found out that over 90% of all households use hired labor while it is a very small proportion who uses own labor for farming. In the light of this, it would be appropriate to investigate the reasons for the intensity of hired labor including the sources of hired labor and the implication thereof in terms of stabilizing already established livelihood systems.

8. *Irrigation:* Irrigation practices either using water from dams (20%) or rivers (53%), is modestly practiced in the study area. Consequently there is a need to investigate the role of irrigation in terms of improving livelihood and how those who engage in the practice differ from the rest in terms of level of income, quality of life and food security.

9. *Poor breeds of livestock and poor veterinary services*: Though households in the sample *woredas* have high possession of livestock, the number of improved varieties is very small. It is, therefore, imperative to know the reasons for low availability of improved varieties as the reasons could be related to lack of capacity on the part of farmers to purchase improved varieties or limited supply of the breeds in the locality. Similarly, it is only 60% of the farmers who sought veterinary services despite the prevalence of animal diseases in the *woredas*. It is, therefore, in order to inquire further and identify the alternatives used when faced with animal diseases. In addition, responding to the query on listing problems adversely affecting livestock production in order of severity, informants enumerated lack of grazing land, paucity of animal feed, absence of adequate vetrinary services, shortage of water, and lack of quality and improved breed as 1st, 2nd, 3rd, 4th, and 5th respectively. In the light of this, subsequent monitoring of state of affairs through periodic studies may indicate whether problems negatively affecting livestock ownership and production are alleviated or not following the intervention of the project.

10. *Information and communication technologies in rural areas*: Nearly one-third of the farmers in the study areas reported possession of telephones and 22% have reported possession of radios. As these items are important sources of information and communication, it might be useful to study their effects on access to markets and livelihoods of the households in the study area

11. *Ownership of productive assets:* The major and outstanding physical assets owned by respondent farming households are houses and livestock

possessed by 98% and 96% of the sample population respectively. With the exception of traditional farming tools and jewelry, no productive asset that is worth mentioning was reported as being possessed by informants. In this regard, one of the focus areas of future studies would be to establish changes and continuities regarding ownership of assets following and resulting from the intervention of the project. It could be argued that if such a lamentable situation regarding ownership of productive assets continue to persist unabated, prospects for economic growth and poverty reduction in the localities under study will be questionable.

12. *Rural housing*: In terms of conditions relating to ownership of houses, the study has established that 90% of the total respondents possess tin-roofed houses. Of these 75% are with two rooms, 51% have separate kitchens, and 50% are places where spouses and children share the same bed implying over-crowding and questionable hygienic conditions. The intervention of the project in improving such a dismal situation is thus envisaged to be one of the major areas of inquiry during future studies.

13. *Alternative forms of livelihood:* Sharecropping, leasing land for oxen, wage employment, renting land from those who are not able to work on it, etc., constitute the major means of alternative access and livelihood in the study areas. Studies on progress of state of affairs to be conducted in subsequent years are hoped to look into aspects of change and continuity with regard to the aforementioned.

14. *Rural saving:* Saving has been reported by 23% of the households or a little more than one-fifth of the population. Though the identified purpose of saving is mainly for household consumption, the practice of saving can stimulate investment. As a result, it is critical to understand what differentiates those who save from those who do not in terms of production capacity, education capability etc in order to identify the determinants of rural savings and use them as instrument to stimulate saving in the study *woreda*.

15. *Rural urban linkages:* Rural urban linkage in the sample *woredas* is limited and farmers visit towns only for buying and selling purposes. Towns, however, are expected to serve the surrounding population as service centers and should provide employment opportunities. It is really necessary to understand why towns in the study area are not playing such roles and do not exhibit stronger linkage with the rural hinterland.

    More specifically the study found that the majority of informants in the five woredas visit urban areas on a biweekly basis to buy and sell commodities, engage in wage labor, access medical and administrative services. The mode of transport to travel to town by the respondents is on foot, which on the average takes 75 minutes with variations from place to place. It is envisaged that the positive ramifications resulting from the intervention of the project might lead to more frequent interaction between rural and urban areas and reduce the burden of traveling on foot for a longer duration. It is thus hoped that subsequent studies will research future trends of change and/or continuity regarding the existing state of affairs relating to rural-urban linkages

16. *Rural non-farm activities*: The study found out that the proportion of households engaged in non-farm activities is 19%. There is, however, a significant variation among *woredas* in this regard. Mecha (45%) and Fogera (22%) have a higher proportion of households earning income from non-farm activities. It appears important to identify the factors which account for such differences among *woredas*. Further, it is also important to study the consequences of non-farm income for those participating in the activity

17. *Health and nutrition:* Nearly 80% of the respondents think their health situation and that of their family members is very good and good and hence the need for medical treatment is absent. On the other hand, 10% are of the view that their health status is poor due to malarial infection, cough, tuberculosis, and typhus in descending order of severity. A total of 6% of the respondents stated that they have experienced maternal death caused due to unassisted child delivery, attempted abortion, and lack of access to proper medical services. As regards providers of medical services, a majority of 57% reported that they were provided with care by government establishments like clinics, health centers and health posts. Child vaccination was undertaken by 73% of the informants in the study locations. In spite of this, however, examination of aspects of change and continuity in regard to the health status of households in subsequent years following the intervention of the project would be the concern of similar studies in subsequent years. Moreover, it was learnt that 76% of the respondent households consume three meals per day while the remaining 24% are limited to one or two meals a day. In view of the situation in rural Ethiopia, the nutrition value of the meals is highly questionable given that the data on the subject indicate that the overwhelming majority rarely have such items like meat in their meals. Incidence of food shortage affecting respondents' families in 2004 EC was reported by 10% of the informants in the study woredas with some variation regarding the degree and extent of shortage from woreda to woreda. Concerning coping

mechanisms on the part of those who experienced shortage, sale of livestock and borrowing from friends and relatives were mentioned as the major means.

Whether improvements in the health and food status of farming households in the project areas are likely to occur as a result of the subsequent interventions of the project would be an issue that is worth examining in the subsequent phases of conducting similar studies.

18. *Rural income and expenditure:* Data on rural household income and expenditure for 2004 EC is elicited in the course of conducting the baseline study. By and large, it was learnt that the major sources of income revolve around sale of agricultural products and livestock and livestock and poultry products while of expenditure in cludes and purchase of crops, animals, tea/coffee, cooking oil, and industrial products on the other. Accordingly, sale of agricultural products by respondent households in 2004 EC include crops like oats, wheat, maize and teff in descending order of average value and revenue obtained. On the other hand, barley and sorghum were sold fetching the least in terms of average value and quantity in descending order of price during the year in question. As regards sale of animals and animal products including poultry, sale of oxen, equines, goats and cows, and butter, eggs, and hides and skin stand prominent in terms of average value in descending order of prices fetched. Expenditures incurred by respondent households in 2004 on crops include maize, millet and pepper in terms of average value and descending order of the amount of money expended whereas purchase of animals relates to cows and heifers in the same order. Moreover, variations in terms of earning income from engagement in non-farm activities in the form of wage employment and sale of firewood and handicraft products were reported by an average of 19% of the informants approached in the woredas under study as sources of non-regular revenue earning. It is hoped that monitoring aspects of change and continuity in regard to the state of income and expenditure highlighted in the foregoing discussion will be one of the focal areas for future research.

19. *Female headed households in urban areas*: Though there is some variation, the study towns revealed that there is significant female headship in the area. This points to the need to study differences and similarity between female and male headed households in their livelihoods, assets and income.

20. *Self employment:* Self-employed people are not evenly distributed among the study towns. Some towns such as Qoladiba (21%), Maksegnit (25%),

and Addis Zemen (26%) have relatively higher proportion of self-employed people. One of the reasons could be that these towns do provide opportunities for self-employment compared to other towns while another reason could be that the surroundings of these towns are poorly suited for farming and hence people have to resort to self employment instead of farming etc. Which of these or other factors underlie self employment need to be known.

21. *Migration:* The study towns are dominated by migrants as significant proportion of the residents were not born in the towns. It was also indicated that economic reasons are the main reason for migration. It might be interesting to follow the migrants and identify how they perform in their livelihood compared to the non-migrants in the destination areas.

22. *Unemployment in towns*: The survey showed that a significant proportion of those who are not currently working are students. In Bahirdar, however, 13% reported that they are not working mainly because they cannot get work. This is an indication that in big towns such as Bahirdar unemployment is high and there is a need to study the causes and possible solutions out of the unemployment situation seen in this town

23. *Employment in businesses*: Businesses in the study towns hire very few people. For example it is only 53 business people who reported that they hire labor in their businesses. The average number of employees in each business is 1.7 or nearly 2 persons. This is an indication that most businesses in the locality are run by the owners with little employment opportunity for others. It is thus important to study why businesses absorb very low number of person or how to revitalize businesses and make them dynamic and sustainable and increase their labor absorbing capacity.

24. *Business income*: The most important use of earnings from business is for household expense (71%). It is only 11% of the businesses which use business income for asset accumulation particularly for buying houses and only 8% for investment. To the extent that most households use business income for consumption, the use of earnings for business growth is very limited. As a result, future research could focus on identifying possible reasons for observed pattern and how to influence business owners to invest in business

25. *Service access:* Some respondents have indicated that they have some difficulty accessing primary school, secondary school and health services. It will be interesting to know who these people are in terms of their socio

economic status and help them solve these problems and increase their access.

26. *Saving and credit*: The proportion of urban households reporting some saving is 31% against 69% who reported to have no savings. A research on the determinants of savings will help influence policy to encourage savings and increase availability of resources for investment. Similarly, it is only 6% who reported borrowing from different sources. It will be interesting to know the reason why only very few people reported borrowing

27. *Rural investment:* The survey showed that it is only 14% of the urban households who reported investing in rural areas. Investing in rural areas is critical since it helps farming to be more productive and more yielding. It is, there fore, important to study the factors that hinder rural investment by urban households.

References

African Development Bank (2001). Koga rrigation and Watershed Management Project available at www.afdb.org/fileadmin/uploads/afdb/document /project

Ministry of Water Resources. (2008) Tana and Beles Integrated Water Resources Development Project: Project Implementation manual, unpublished

Ministry of Water Resources (2010a) Tana Beles Integrated Project document, unpublished

Ministry of Water Resource (2010b). Environmental and Social Impact Assessment of the Rib Irrigation and Drainage Project, AA available at www.mowr.gov.et/attachementfiles/downloads/RIDP_ESIA _Vol.11.pdf

MoFED (2006). A plan for Accelerated and Sustainable Development to End Poverty (PASDEP) Vol. 1 main text, Addis Ababa.

World Bank (2010). Environmental and Social Impact Assessment of the Megech Pump (Seraba) Irrigation and Drainage Project, Addis Ababa.

www.ingramcontent.com/pod-product-compliance
Lightning Source LLC
Chambersburg PA
CBHW081739270326
41932CB00020B/3329
9789994450497